RENAISSANCE MEN AND IDEAS

ROBERT SCHWOEBEL
editor

RENAISSANCE MEN AND IDEAS

ST. MARTIN'S PRESS
New York

AFFILIATED PUBLISHERS: Macmillan & Company, Limited, London—also at
Bombay, Calcutta, Madras and Melbourne; The Macmillan Company of Canada,
Limited, Toronto.

🎑 Preface

These essays on important men and ideas of the Renaissance enlarge upon issues that are usually met only fleetingly in textbooks. Prepared especially for this volume, they aim to provide factual and analytical materials for reflection and discussion. The emphasis of most of the essays on Renaissance assumptions and values will make them useful guides to students reading *The Prince, Utopia, The Book of the Courtier,* the *Commentaries* of Pius II, Montaigne's *Essays,* or the works of Petrarch, Valla, Luther, and Copernicus.

This collection also seeks to bridge the ever-widening gap between the world of the specialized scholar and that of the undergraduate student, between the scholarly journal and the textbook. The contributors are well known for their work in these particular fields. As specialists, however, they have directed their previous studies primarily to fellow scholars. In writing these essays (and in the public lectures as which all but the first of them originated), the authors have paused to take a fresh look at their subject and to address themselves specifically to an audience of undergraduates.

This collection gives the student a glimpse of the scholar at work and of the process by which our understanding of the past is continuously revised. The contributors were at liberty to emphasize any aspect of their subject. They were encouraged nevertheless to produce a synthesis that would take into account the pertinent work of other scholars as well as their own original work. And their knowledge of past and current controversies in Renaissance historiography allows them freely to interpret the lives and works of the outstanding individuals that are their concern, thus inducing us to reexamine the conventional interpretations of the period.

The study of history is made attractive and meaningful when it is approached as the study of people. These essays analyze Renaissance thought and sentiment in the light of the distinctive characters and personalities that shaped them. The figures dealt with here were all more or less prominent in their own time, and their importance, their "contributions," are duly acknowledged. They are presented, however, not as heroes but as mortals, as men with anxieties and fears as well as courage, with shortcomings as well as unusual talents, with insecurities as well as ambitions— and thus as men not so different from the rest of us.

For their assistance and support in organizing the Renaissance program at Temple University I wish to thank Professor C. William Miller and Miss Tobey Gordon. I am also grateful to the Trustees of Temple University for underwriting the program. For their helpful criticism of the editorial work and the introduction to this volume, I am indebted to Professor William Rauch, my colleague in the History Department at Temple, and to Mr. Colwyn Krussman, a former colleague.

🎔 Contents

Introduction

In turning to the Renaissance the student is confronted with one of the rich and exciting periods in the history of western civilization. The fall of Constantinople, the invention of printing from moveable type, the publication of Luther's ninety-five theses—a mere listing of the best known events suggests the dramatic character of the times. Bounded at one end by Dante and Petrarch and at the other by Shakespeare, encompassing the lives and careers of painters, sculptors, and architects whose names are legendary, the Renaissance was, in art and literature, one of the great creative eras in Western civilization. It was, at the same time, the beginning of the European age in world history: the discovery of America, Da Gama's opening of the sea route around Africa to the Orient, and the circumnavigation of the globe by Magellan's expedition—all took place within three decades.

But the Renaissance was also a restless and chaotic era, a period of accelerating change, and of discontinuity. It experienced sharp demographic fluctuations and severe, recurrent economic and social dislocations. War, disease, hunger were constant scourges, with poverty, repression, and bigotry far more prevalent than wealth or individual freedom or toleration. For the great majority life was brief, harsh, and materially unrewarding. Many of its most imaginative and creative efforts were abortive or short-lived. Promising leaders turned tyrants. Champions of human rights and liberty of conscience condemned and killed their opponents. Joan of Arc, John Hus, Savonarola were burned for what they believed. Henry VIII murdered royal wives and his lord chancellor, Thomas More. Protestants and Catholics massacred each other while they nursed a common enmity for Jews and Turks.

An age as agitated and complex as the Renaissance is bound to give rise to conflicting interpretations. For more than a century now it has been a battleground for historians. The initial attack was delivered by the historians of the Middle Ages, who tried to demonstrate that the creative impulses of the Renaissance were all spawned during the Middle Ages or that the Renaissance was the Indian summer of medieval civilization. In a daring frontal assault one group endeavored to obliterate the Renaissance altogether by denying that it had ever existed!

This controversy (aspects of which are touched upon in the following essays) can be traced back to the Renaissance itself. Indeed the arguments of modern scholars often seem to echo the diverse reactions of Renaissance men to their own times, for they too argued about the meaning of their age. They too wondered whether their time marked the end of an old or the beginning of a new order. Vast changes on and beyond their borders (the rise of the Ottoman Turks, the fall of Byzantium, the discovery of new lands), forced them to revise established notions about the place of Europe in the world. New knowledge of non-Christian civilizations caused them to reflect upon and question their western cultural tradition, while unsettling changes inside Europe (the collapse of medieval structures and the rise of new social and economic forces) made them aware of the distinctiveness of their own era and provoked discussion about its place in the scheme of universal history.

Social changes within Renaissance Europe brought new structures and new life styles — an urban, lay culture, commercial economy, the power state, and dynastic monarchies. Old values and virtues no longer reflected the realities of social life. Renaissance man was hard put to reconcile the professed ideals of the received tradition and the way people actually lived. The creative and vital forces of the new culture were located in towns and cities that were centers of commerce, industry, banking. Renaissance culture was essentially a civic and commercial culture. Yet the proponents of a traditional Christian ethic proclaimed the value of the ascetic life. The ideal Christian was one who lived apart from the world and who pursued neither wealth nor worldly renown.

The conservative tradition asserted also the virtue of the contemplative life. The highest calling of the scholar was that of learned leisure. Detached and withdrawn from the pressures of worldly affairs, the man of learning was best able to reflect and meditate on truly important matters such as the imminence of death. The conflict between the ethical requirements laid down by the Catholic church and the demands and obligations of a responsible civic life was the source of widespread anxiety and emotional turmoil. For the Renaissance scholar and thinker, this conflict was also the source of much intellectual controversy. Adherents of the new learning, what we call Renaissance humanism, were convinced that scholars and writers had a definite function to perform in the life of society. They even denounced those intellectual disciplines which had grown too theoretical and failed to deal with the practical and ethical concerns of man.

Not the least of the problems that Renaissance intellectuals and all concerned people had to wrestle with was the development of the state. During the fourteenth century and much of the fifteenth, Europe was convulsed with political anarchy that paved the way for the rise of despots, urban oligarchies, and dynastic princes and monarchs. These political creatures were the architects of the power state. They were successful because they could mobilize and wield power. And their power derived from effective organization and exploitation of the disparate forces and resources of society — aristocracy, merchants, the church (Catholic and Protestant), agriculture. From these sources the rulers obtained the extraordinary revenue (revenue in addition to the rents and dues that accrued to them from their own holdings), with which they paid their professional troops, administrations, lawyers, diplomats and their hand-picked church leaders.

Because it worked, that is because it became the best guarantee of internal order and security and endeavored to create the conditions necessary for economic prosperity, the new state received widespread support. But the Renaissance ruler sometimes gained his position and frequently maintained it by means that conflicted with established notions about the proper behavior of those called upon to rule. Neither King Ferdinand in Spain, nor Henry VIII of

England, nor any other successful monarch of the time fitted very well the humanist conception of the ruler as a benevolent and just prince cast in the image of Christ. How was Renaissance man to justify the pursuit and exercise of power, as described in the writings of Machiavelli and practiced by the rulers of his day, with the widespread belief that the prince existed to dispense justice? What in fact was the proper relationship between the ruler and his people? The ruler and the law? The secular prince and the church? In order to insure the continuation of the dynasty, a source of stability and continuity in government, was it legitimate for Henry VIII to divorce Catherine of Aragon? Was it right that he, or the king of France, or the king of Spain, or the princes in Germany determine the fortunes of the church in their lands?

Change in all areas of Renaissance society evoked questions equally profound and perplexing. Men were impelled to question, to search for a new theory of values, a new moral authority. This search for values is an essential aspect of the historical life of any culture. It is the means by which each age arrives at its own explanation and understanding of itself and of its place in human history. For in human affairs it is not just action and events which make history. No less important are the reasons, the justifications that men ascribe to activity, the meaning that they attribute to it.

This book is about ten men who played a significant part in the Renaissance search for meaning. In their special areas of interest—politics, religion, science, literature, manners—they worried about and reflected on the conflict of old values and new ways. In books, some of which have become classics—*The Prince, Utopia, The Book of the Courtier, Essays*—they discussed questions which troubled their times and still trouble ours: the nature and uses of power; the responsibility and possibility of education; the limits of reason; the sources of moral authority; the social and ethical implications of scientific discovery and new technology.

Nine of the ten are well known today and were more or less famous in their own period. The tenth, Albrecht von Eyb, was known to a limited audience then and is familiar to only a handful of scholars now. The years spanned by the lives of the ten comprise almost exactly the three centuries of the Renaissance. Petrarch, the earliest, was born in 1304; the last, Montaigne, died in 1592. All were Europeans. Petrarch, Valla, Pius II, Machiavelli, and Castiglione were Italians. Luther and Eyb were German. More was English, Montaigne was from France, and Copernicus was born in Poland. Since the essays do not deal with the entire careers of these men, a short introduction to each of them may be useful.

The life of Francesco Petrarca or, as we call him, Petrarch, was entirely one of study, of observing the world, of reflection and writing. Born at Arezzo, he spent his earliest years on his father's estates at Incisa, and lived briefly at Pisa. When he was eight his family left Italy and followed the papal court to southern France. (In 1309 the papacy, owing chiefly to troubled relations with the French king, had settled in Avignon, where it remained until 1377.) Petrarch was educated in France and Italy, studying law and hating it until his father's death freed him to follow his literary interests.

To support a literary career, Petrarch, like many contemporary artists and writers, sought and served wealthy patrons at the papal court. Although he frequently visited Italy, for the next quarter of a century his life centered around Avignon. It was during these years that he wrote his best poetry, including those poems inspired by the mysterious lady Laura whom Petrarch loved, presumably at a distance. In 1352–53 he left France for good, still in search of the perfect patron, one who would grant him the leisure and independence he regarded as indispensable for his work. He spent the last twenty years of his life at various Italian courts and towns, including Milan, Venice, Padua, and Pavia. He died in his own house at Arquà in 1374, the most famous man of letters in Europe of his generation.

In contrast to the academic humanists of today, Petrarch had no interest in scholarship for its own sake. Indeed he reserved his most scornful criticism for the academicians of his own time, the professors of law, medicine, philosophy, and theology. As Petrarch saw it they were preoccupied with useless abstractions and irrelevant trivialities. Study and learning, he believed, must be related to real life; they must speak to the human condition, to the whole man, not just to his rational process.

In defense of his position he cited the authority of ancient Roman writers like Cicero. Petrarch believed that the glory of Rome was due in no small part to its literary culture. In the age of Cicero, rhetoric, poetry, and history were highly esteemed. The orator, one educated in the art of communication, and in history, poetry, and moral philosophy, had occupied a position of prominence in society. Properly so, Petrarch asserted, for such studies instructed those capacities in man which made for greatness. In antiquity they informed the will and spirit of the Romans and helped to shape the indomitable Roman character.

Petrarch was certain that his own times would profit by emulating the example of the ancients. He was greatly distressed by the condition of society in the fourteenth century—the political anarchy, social unrest, decline of the church, the debased state of culture. He therefore took upon himself the task of restoring the educational and cultural values of the ancient Roman literary tradition. No doubt he perceived his own role by analogy with that of the Roman orators he so admired. He certainly searched for manuscripts of classical authors with great vigor, and let no opportunity pass to publicize his cause. Through personal contacts—he was one of those people who knew everybody—he stimulated a widespread interest in the classics. Through his studies, his extensive correspondence, and an impressive list of prose and poetical works, he succeeded, almost single-handedly, in bringing classical studies to a position of prominence in the new culture of the Renaissance. Whether he succeeded in awakening his contemporaries to a new vision of man and a new system of values is a question much discussed today.

Lorenzo Valla (1407–1457) was one of the truly brilliant humanists of Renaissance Italy. He grew up in Rome, served as private secretary to the king of Naples, and spent the last decade of his life at the papal court. Valla surpassed Petrarch and most of his own contemporaries not only in his knowledge of classical Greek and Latin but in his mastery of the science of language. Like Petrarch, however, he believed that learning was to be put to practical purposes, to advance understanding and to improve the quality of life in society. Throughout his career Valla acted on his convictions. Possessing the unusual combination of genius, the disciplined skills of scholarship, a profound moral commitment, and personal courage, he was constantly involved in controversy. He was a ruthless critic of those whom he regarded as the authors of ignorance, bigotry, or false learning. Abrasive, cocky, and usually right, he attacked without mercy or modesty fellow humanists, orthodox churchmen, medieval writers, and early church fathers. In return he was denounced as a pagan and charged with heresy; and though both claims were false, Valla has enjoyed a dubious reputation ever since.

The best known example of Valla's work is his *Treatise on the Donation of Constantine*. In this he attacked the right of the papacy to rule over its lands in Italy. Through the application of philology and historical learning he demonstrated that the document on which the papal claims were based was a medieval forgery. Similarly it was on the basis of his knowledge of language and history that Valla attacked what he regarded as bad translations by St. Jerome, the early church father who had produced the Vulgate, the standard Latin text of the Bible.

The prime target of Valla's criticism, however, was the theological tradition the church had inherited from the Middle Ages. He objected vigorously to the uses which Christian theologians since the time of St. Thomas Aquinas had made of the ancient philosophers. Specifically Valla repudiated the validity of ethical precepts derived from the philosophical schools of the ancients. He argued that the appropriate antique source for moral guidance was that of the rhetorical tradition, and claimed that rhetoric, the art of exhortation and of persuasion, was more useful than the abstractions of the philosophers in influencing the behavior of man. Valla believed the conception of man held by the Roman orators to be closer to Christianity than that of the ancient philosophers. Rhetoric was therefore the more appropriate source for the moral guidance of Christians.

Albrecht von Eyb (1420–1475) was first educated in his native Germany at Erfurt and Rothenburg. He went on to Italy, where he studied at Pavia and Bologna, receiving his doctorate in law from the former in the year 1459. Upon returning to Germany Eyb occupied a number of ecclesiastical offices, practiced what we would call international law, and served as counselor to the Margrave of Brandenburg. Although occupied with an active career in church and secular government, he found time to study and to write. Eyb produced two works, *Margarita poetica (The Pearl of Humanism)*, and *Ehebuch (Book of Marriage)*, which were widely read in Renaissance Germany.

Eyb's literary career substantiates the fact that the humanistic culture of the Renaissance took root in Germany earlier than is usually claimed. Containing selections from the ancient orators and the Italian humanists, his *Pearl of Humanism* introduced to Germany not only the art of the ancient rhetoricians but also their ideas and moral standards. The fact that Eyb's work was so popular shows further that there was a significant literate public in Germany receptive to the ideas and sentiments conveyed by the ancient Roman literary tradition.

The work of Eyb further illustrates that there were scholars and printers in Germany who were concerned with disseminating the new learning. In fact the printing history of his books provides us with a concrete demonstration of how the new invention functioned in the production of new social attitudes. Eyb was not satisfied with the success of his first efforts. Though not one of the leading scholars or writers of the Renaissance, he was more committed than many of the famous *literati* to instructing the common people in the values of the new learning. In his *Book of Marriage* Eyb translated into German extracts from the ancients and Renaissance Italian writers. It is clear that the work was intended for the widest possible audience for in his preface he tells us that he intentionally included entertaining stories so that people would want to read it and *hear* it *(zu lesen und zu hören).*

Although humanism took root in England in the early fifteenth century it was not until a century later that it blossomed. The spread of the new culture there is rightly associated with the name of Thomas More (1478–1535), who for a quarter of a century was one of its leading lights. Among the men discussed in this book, More alone held high office in a civil government, serving as Lord Chancellor under Henry VIII from 1529 until 1532. In the latter year he retired, finding himself unable to sanction the divorce of King Henry from Catherine of Aragon. His former friendship with the king and his reputation as a humanist scholar were not sufficient to save his life when he refused to accept the separation of the English church from Rome and its subjugation to the will and authority of the crown. Tried and convicted of treason, More gained immortality in history and sainthood in the Roman Catholic church by courageously holding to his convictions and bravely meeting his death.

As a Renaissance scholar and writer More is inevitably associated with the Dutchman Erasmus, the most famous of the northern humanists. Indeed it is impossible to talk about humanism in England without mentioning Erasmus, who played a decisive role in nurturing among his English friends the pursuit and love of the new learning. It was in More's own house that Erasmus wrote his *Praise of Folly,* the best known of his satirical works in which he criticized the ridiculous, demeaning, and dehumanizing habits of his contemporaries. More's equally famous *Utopia* was certainly inspired by the friendship of its author with Erasmus.

More and Erasmus were committed to basically the same values and prescribed the same cures for the ills of their contemporaries. Although they espoused the humane values of the ancient literary culture, they were essentially conservative in their conception of society and their notion of reform. Both saw the salvation of man and society as resting ultimately with the church. The lay ruler must do his part. As a loyal son of the church he should set an example. As a Christian prince it was his duty to defend the faith and to provide justice for his subjects.

But at the end of the fifteenth and in the sixteenth centuries, as More and Erasmus viewed it, neither church nor prince were performing as they were supposed to. If the prince was enhancing his personal power by plundering the church, the church itself was failing in its duty and acting increasingly like a secular regime. Thus the church was incapable of achieving the renovation of society until it first undertook to reform itself. By reform More and Erasmus meant bringing the life and practices of the church into greater conformance with the ideals of the Sermon on the Mount. Scholarship was to contribute to the reform by the reclamation and study of the earliest sources of Christianity—the New Testament and the writings of the church fathers. Both men believed in the educability of their fellow man. Both believed that men were responsible for their actions and had a hand in shaping their destiny. They expected that when men were informed of the true teachings of Christ and guided by a purified and enlightened church, they would not fail to respond.

More, like Erasmus, was wholly dedicated to reforms within the church. He was appalled, as his polemical and theological treatises demonstrate, by the thought of destroying the existing institution in order to bring about improvement. It was his devotion to the institutional church under the authority of the pope which brought More to his downfall and death. In refusing to accept the crown's claim to authority over the church, More stood on the side of tradition and in opposition to the most revolutionary trend of the Renaissance, the emergence of the absolutist state.

Of all the great Renaissance names, only that of Niccolo Machiavelli (1469–1527) is a household word today. He was certainly not so prominent in his own lifetime. He was not a member of the ruling class of his native Florence. His post as second chancellor and secretary in the Florentine chancery was that of an important civil servant. His job was to carry out the policy made by others. The years in which he saw public service (1498–1512) were, however, a critical time in the history of Florence and all Italy. And the events of these years were not lost on Machiavelli, who drew upon his own experience and knowledge of them when in forced retirement he produced the writings on politics on which his fame rests.

Four years before Machiavelli entered the government of Florence, the French king Charles VIII invaded Italy. The invasion initiated a chain of political reactions which among other things included the fall of the Medici regime in Florence, Italy's losing control of her own destiny, the establishment of France and Spain in the Italian peninsula, and the alliance of Spain and the Holy Roman Empire in longstanding opposition to France. The republic which Machiavelli served came into being in the wake of the invasion of 1494. Between then and its fall in 1512 much time was spent in trying to create the perfect system of government in Florence and restore the city to the position which it had held in Tuscany prior to the French invasion. Unable to control the forces and events which now determined the fortunes of Italy, the new government succumbed when the Medici were restored by the army of the Holy League, an alliance of powers organized by Pope Julius II.

Machiavelli was no happier than most Italians about the misfortunes which visited the peninsula. But his reaction was significantly different. Out of a job, but hoping to find a position with the new regime, he wrote *The Prince*. Machiavelli was conscious of the novelty of the work. He believed that he was providing a scientific analysis of the practice of government based on experience and on the study of the past. He went beyond events and analyzed the characteristic behavior of men and institutions. His conclusions were stark and shocking. He said in effect that the way things had gone in Italy constituted political reality. And he went on to prescribe what the rulers of Florence must do in order to survive and prosper within that reality.

Machiavelli understood and accepted the Renaissance phenomenon of the power state. In this respect *The Prince* is a reflection of developments in the political world of the time. But for Machiavelli it was not sufficient merely to describe political practice as it then stood. For him, and for the prince if he were to succeed, it was necessary to examine and grasp the underlying motives of behavior. Machiavelli concluded that men and states were equally aggressive, ambitious, grasping. Change, disorder, and struggle were facts of life. To project policies on the basis of what man ought to be was to court disaster. The ruler had to be able to control those forces which directly affected the success of his plans. To accomplish his aims he had to possess the necessary power.

Faith, trust, and good will were illusions. He depended finally on his own resources and on the strength which he commanded.

Machiavelli claimed that his sole concern was with politics. In submitting political activity to systematic study and extracting the basic principles on which it operated, he felt he was doing for politics what others had recently done for painting or architecture. He left to others the problem of working out the implications of his findings as they related to other functions in society.

On the walls of the cathedral library in Siena one can still review the career of Aeneas Sylvius Piccolomini (b. 1405), who became Pius II (1458–1464) in the ten frescoes done by Pinturicchio in the early sixteenth century. From a poor but noble family of Siena, Aeneas studied law and literature and was fitted equally for service in secular government or in the church. The first three frescoes show the progress of his career: starting out as secretary to a bishop on his way to the council of Basel; on a mission to Scotland concerning that country's relations with England vis-à-vis the Hundred Years War; his service at the court of the German emperor, Frederick III, who rewards him with the laurel crown of the poet. Two frescoes depict important missions which Aeneas carried out for the emperor: the reconciliation of the latter with the pope after a rupture of their relations at the time of the council of Basel; and Aeneas introducing Frederick to his future bride, Eleanora of Portugal, a union which he had helped arrange. Five frescoes then show the career of the churchman: Aeneas receiving the red hat of a cardinal; his entering St. John the Lateran as the newly elected Pope Pius II; the opening of the congress of Mantua; Pius canonizing St. Catherine of Siena; and the last, Pius at Ancona where he had gone to lead the crusade but where he died.

The frescoes do more than portray the major events in the life of Pius. Pinturicchio made his preliminary sketches while reading the biography of the pope by his secretary Campano and Pius' own *Commentaries*. The scenes present those things for which Pius himself, and his nephew, who commissioned the work, wished the pope to be remembered. They reveal the ideals and aspirations which Pius announced in his lifetime as the basis of his deeds. Thus the frescoes show him working for church reform, peace among Christian princes, the unity of Christendom, the recognition of the universal authority of pope and emperor, and the defense of the faith.

Later generations and even some contemporary critics of the papacy might see attitudes expressed in the frescoes which they

would not regard as praiseworthy. The scenes are entirely aristocratic in tone. The fact was that Pius disliked commoners, hated
merchants, and had a low opinion of those governments in which
either participated. Similarly his conception of the church was
aristocratic and hierarchic. Pius was not to forget that as a layman
he had attended the reform council of Basel which operated on the
basis of the conciliar notion of church government as representing
and its authority as deriving from the whole body of the church.
Basel had failed miserably to deal with the reform of fiscal and
administrative matters. It had practiced the same abuses it condemned in the papacy. It had failed to prosecute the crusade, solve
the problem of heresy, and bring unity and concord to Christendom. Instead, under the influence of radicals, ordinary priests and
laymen who insisted on participating, it had created schism. When
he attended Basel Pius had been both a layman and an adherent
of the conciliar position. But his experience there ended in strength-
ening his aristocratic sentiments and his fears of popular move-
ments. His commitment to reform was to be in the conservative
tradition as represented by Rome. And Rome was not a vantage
point from which to understand the new directions and tendencies
of Renaissance society.

Martin Luther (1483–1546) is rightly remembered first as a
man of religious faith, "a religious genius," as he has been called,
and then for his central role in the religious revolt of the sixteenth
century. As the Reformation was the result of many different
forces—political, social, economic, intellectual—so too Luther
must be understood in light of the diverse tendencies at work in
his time. But in either case, Reformation or Luther, religion was at
the center. Luther found the answer to the riddle of life in the
Bible. His role as reformer was an act of faith. He spoke to the
people about religious reform. And he was distressed when his
words were interpreted to apply to the social situation in Germany
by the peasants and others.

Certainly Luther thought of himself as a man of God, as a religious being. At the same time, however, he understood his occupation, his vocation, as he put it, to be that of a scholar, specifically
a Biblical scholar and professor. As such Luther represented an
amalgam of the intellectual currents of the Renaissance. A student
and teacher of the Holy Scriptures, he was learned in the Biblical
scholarship handed down from the church fathers and the Middle
Ages and greatly enriched by Renaissance scholars such as Valla
and Erasmus. Luther was well acquainted with the theological

schools which had interpreted the meaning of Christianity for the church. Although not a humanist, either in the professional sense or in his view of man, he drew heavily upon the distinctive approach of the humanists in dealing with sacred literature as well as on the philological skills which they had developed. Luther, however, always insisted upon the intervention of the Holy Spirit as essential for understanding the true meaning of the Bible. For us it is essential to appreciate the work of Luther the scholar if we are to understand his role as religious reformer.

The basic facts which comprise the biography of Nicholas Copernicus (1473-1543) belie the revolution which issued from the life work of this creative but modest scholar. He began his studies in mathematics and astronomy at the university of Cracow, then spent ten years studying in Italy at Bologna, Padua, and Ferrara, taking a doctorate in canon law at the latter. Having in the meantime been appointed a canon in the cathedral of Frauenburg he returned, in 1506, to his native Ermeland (East Prussia), which then belonged to Poland. From 1506 to 1512, Copernicus served the bishop of Ermeland in his see at Heilsberg. He aided the bishop in the government and administration of his diocese and was also his personal physician. When the bishop died in 1512, Copernicus finally assumed his position as canon in Frauenburg, where he remained until his death in 1543.

There was nothing in any of this to suggest that Copernicus was to publish the most revolutionary teaching of his day. There is reason to believe that if he had been left to himself, Copernicus would not have revealed his work except to a few trusted friends. A key role in bringing his work to light was played by a young Christian scholar, Georg Joachim Rhaeticus (1514-76) who, though a Lutheran, traveled from Wittenberg, where he was a professor in the university, to Frauenburg. He worked for two years with Copernicus and then saw to the printing of the latter's work in several stages. The final text of the *De revolutionibus* was printed at Nuremberg, and an advance copy of it reached Copernicus on his deathbed.

Copernicus did not live to see the theological storm raised by his work. For scientists the astronomer's data and demonstrations proved beyond question that the sun and not the earth was the center of the solar system. Suddenly the earth had become one of the heavenly bodies. How were Christians to deal with this finding? Copernicus was a loyal Catholic and an ecclesiastical administrator. His work had been encouraged by three Catholic bishops, one cardinal, and two popes, and he had been assisted by a Lutheran. Copernicus the astronomer seemed content to allow others to wrestle with the theological and moral implications of his work.

The best introduction to *The Book of the Courtier* is an account of the life of its author. All authorities agree that Baldasare Castiglione (1478–1529) was himself a prime example of the ideal courtier about whom he wrote. Born on his family estates at Casatico near Mantua, Castiglione studied at Milan, where he received his introduction to court life under Duke Ludovico Sforza. After a few years at the court of Mantua, where he got his first taste of military action, he established himself in the service of Duke Guidobaldo di Montefeltro of Urbino. Located on the eastern slopes of the Apennines, midway down the peninsula, Urbino was one of the few smaller places in Italy that had maintained its independence, mainly because it was useful as such to the larger powers. It was here that Castiglione entered into the full range of court activities: intellectual exercises, horsemanship, music, painting, poetry, military feats, etc. All that he describes in *The Book of the Courtier* was supposed to have transpired there on four consecutive days in March 1507.

Castiglione remained in the service of Urbino until 1513. During this time he was active in the business of the court and represented the duke on missions to Henry VII of England and to the French king, Louis XII. In 1513 he briefly entered the service of Pope Leo X in Rome, at which time it is believed he wrote most of his book on court life. He was in Rome again as the representative of Mantua in 1521, during the last days of Leo X, when he became the friend of both the pope and the artist Raphael, and spent his last five years as papal representative of Clement VII to the court of Charles V in Spain. When he died in Toledo in 1529, Charles V was reported to have announced to his courtiers: "I tell you one of the finest gentlemen in the world is dead."

Castiglione's work is one of the sources from which we draw the notion that the Renaissance was concerned with the perfection of man. Clearly, without denying the divine source of man's power, Castiglione was concerned with demonstrating human worthiness, man's potential to educate himself, his ability to accomplish that to which he put his mind, to regulate his passions in order to achieve a measured existence. But in *The Book of the Courtier* he did not address himself to all men; the world of Castiglione was wholly that of the Renaissance court. It was peopled with princes and nobles. It was under the aegis of the prince that one entered into a full life. Castiglione accepted the Renaissance state as a *fait accompli*. His advice to his aristocratic readers was to cultivate the life of gentility and to educate themselves in order to be of service to their prince.

Michel de Montaigne (1533–1592), owing to his father's progressive ideas about education, was, as an infant, put in the home of a peasant in order to learn humility and simplicity. Under the supervision of a tutor he was prevented from hearing French in his earliest years so that Latin became his first language. For Montaigne, his own personal studies were always paramount. And fortunately, beginning with his father and continuing with his tutor at the Collège de Guyenne in Bordeaux, he came under the supervision of enlightened men who helped him to develop his unique potential and thus to become what it was in him to be — in spite of the fact that he ran into the inanities which too often accompany institutionalized education.

Montaigne's life was not entirely one of study and writing. He served for thirteen years on a tax court that was part of the Parlement of Bordeaux. He was attracted to Paris and to the royal court, and for his services to it at various times he was awarded honors by three French kings, Charles IX, Henry III, and Henry IV. After resigning from the Parlement at the age of thirty-eight, he retired to his estates some thirty miles east of Bordeaux. Here he wrote his *Essays*, Books I and II being published at Bordeaux in 1580. In the midst of the wars of religion in France he was called from retirement to serve for four years as mayor of Bordeaux. Between 1580 and 1588 he completed the third book of the *Essays* and a new edition of the whole work was published in Paris in 1588. Though he continued his relations with King Henry III and, after the latter's assassination, with his successor, Henry IV, from the late 1580's until his death he spent most of his time at home editing and polishing the *Essays*.

Considering the chaotic times in which he lived it is understandable that Montaigne became preoccupied with the problem of determining what it meant to be human and how one was to live accordingly. In the midst of civil turmoil, warring religions, rival intellectual schools, it was no wonder that he concentrated on self-knowledge and emphasized what he regarded as fundamental in humanity—reason, the senses, the will. His search, however, was no retreat from either reality or responsibility. As we have seen he responded to the call of public service, and much against his own personal wishes. For others he stated simply: "The main responsibility of each of us is his own conduct; that is what we are here for."

RENAISSANCE HUMANISM: PETRARCH AND VALLA

Jerrold E. Seigel

Humanism is a word with

many meanings. Like "liberty" and "democracy," "relevance" and "commitment," "humanism" is a slogan that has been attached to many opposing interests and identities. For instance, there is a group in the United States which calls itself the American Humanist Society. Its values seem to come out of the eighteenth century Enlightenment, its hero is Tom Paine, and its cause is atheism. In place of religion, it upholds the values of science. That is one meaning of humanism in our time. In our universities, however, the specific content of humanism seems very different: here the humanists are precisely those who are not scientists, and in at least one major American university, one of the humanistic departments is a Department of Religion. Perhaps these vagaries of meaning suggest why the words of a Roman poet are often chosen as a humanist motto: *Homo sum, nihil humanum a me alienum puto*—I am a man, nothing human is foreign to me. The humanism suggested by this motto is hardly clearly defined: there are so many competing ways of being human. When people proclaim that they are "humanists," it is therefore prudent to question them closely on what they mean. By questioning others on what humanism means or has meant to them, we may discover whether such a protean and overused word can continue to have any significance to us.

The earliest group of people called "humanists" appeared in Europe during the Renaissance. Their central purpose was to revive classical culture. No one then spoke of human*ism*—that word and its equivalents in the various European languages only emerged early in the nineteenth century. But people did speak of human*ists*. The word *umanista* in Italian and similar terms in other languages were in current use around 1500, first of all, it seems, in the slang of university students, who referred in this way to the teachers of a certain group of subjects. The subjects in question had earlier been grouped together under a somewhat more dignified Latin label as *studia humanitatis,* the studies of humanity— or "humanistic studies." The phrase *studia humanitatis* had classical roots, and in using it the teachers of these subjects meant to associate themselves with certain classical thinkers. In Latin the phrase was current by around 1400. At that time Leonardo Bruni, one of the outstanding representatives of early Renaissance humanism, wrote a letter praising the *studia humanitatis* as "those studies which perfect and adorn man." Bruni and his friends certainly thought of these subjects as the basis for some kind of humanism, even though they did not use the word. What did they have in mind?

The precise subjects included in the *studia humanitatis* varied depending on who was making the count, but there was a fair consensus nonetheless. There were usually five such subjects, namely grammar, rhetoric, poetry, history, and moral philosophy. It is an interesting list: consider first of all what it omits. Excluded was the queen discipline of the medieval universities, theology; but absent too was what became the most influential intellectual pursuit of the seventeenth century, natural science (or, as it would have been called in the Renaissance, natural philosophy). That religion and science were not included among the concerns of the humanists does not mean that these subjects were not pursued in the fifteenth century. On the contrary, they were then matters of passionate concern. But in general they were not the primary interests of the humanists. Not all Renaissance thinkers and writers were humanists; some very intelligent and important thinkers would have been insulted to have the name applied to themselves. The humanists were proud of the term, but in using it they expected other people to understand what it included and what it left out.

The five subjects of the *studia humanitatis* had one thing in common: they were all concerned with the life of man in society.

The first two, grammar and rhetoric, are arts of communication; to study them is to study language, to learn to understand the spoken and written word, and to use it oneself. Grammar teaches clarity in speech and writing, while rhetoric strives for effectiveness. Thus grammar and rhetoric are social arts: Robinson Crusoe alone on his island would have no need of either. History and moral philosophy also deal with man in society. Only human communities conscious of their group identity have given birth to histories; only men concerned with their relationship to other men have bothered themselves about what kinds of conduct are ethical and what kinds are not. Grammar and rhetoric deal with communication, history and moral philosophy with action. Poetry stands in between (at least it did for Renaissance men): the poet finds meaning and power in words that other men cannot find; but he also confronts the great deeds and great dilemmas of human life and places them before his audience.

The list of subjects included in the *studia humanitatis* therefore tells us something about what Leonardo Bruni meant when he said that these studies could "perfect and adorn man." Bruni's humanism did not regard a man as perfected and adorned when he devoted himself primarily to his individual well-being, not even his religious well-being, his salvation. Nor did this humanism associate human perfection with man's rational ability to comprehend the workings of the universe. Instead, Bruni's perfected and adorned man was one prepared to take up a life in society together with his fellow men, to communicate with them clearly and effectively, and to understand both the past and the principles on which his community's values were based. If this has a modern ring, there is a reason. Modern life has developed in cities, and many of the human values we cherish have their sources in the development of our highly urbanized civilization. Bruni and his fellow humanists also lived in an urban culture, in the busy and complex towns of 15th century Italy. Bruni himself spent most of his life in Florence, where he held the important office of chancellor. Other humanists had similar positions. Their life, like ours, was formed by the city.

Some things therefore seem reassuringly familiar to us in Renaissance humanism, but there are others that seem disconcertingly strange too. We confront one of these if we ask which of the five *studia humanitatis* seemed the most important to the humanists of the time. This is difficult to answer with certainty, because the humanists gave very fulsome praise to each of the five in turn, but even after we have given scholarly caution its due we have to recognize that the humanists made a curious choice. For them, the central discipline of the *studia humanitatis* was rhetoric. Practically wherever we look in fifteenth-century humanism, we are confronted with the humanist exaltation of rhetoric. This may seem odd to us: Aware that high-flown oratory can be empty at its core, we are suspicious of "mere rhetoric."

The representatives of the *studia humanitatis* regarded rhetoric as the central humanistic discipline for three main reasons. The first is that, steeped in the literature of the ancient world, they were keenly aware of something most of us have forgotten, namely the enormous prestige and importance of rhetoric in classical culture. In the Greek *polis* and the Roman *civitas,* the orator was a figure of great importance. He was influential in political meetings, central to the procedures of the law courts, and prominent at public festivals and celebrations. The Greek word for politician was *rhetor.* In both Greece and Rome, education for public life centered on education in public speaking. But the classical orator claimed an ability to speak on any subject, and his notion of education was encyclopedic. Rhetoric, therefore, was not a merely verbal discipline; its students had to learn to deal with matters of substance too. Since ancient men usually regarded the sum of all knowledge as philosophy (in Greek the word means "love of wisdom"), the classical orator sought to combine rhetoric with philosophy.

In the eyes of the Renaissance humanists, the best exemplar of these ideals in the ancient world was Cicero. Cicero was distinguished in all the varieties of oratory, and his rhetorical gifts helped him in his role as an active and influential Roman statesman. He discussed the education of the orator or future statesman in his treatises, took very seriously the obligation of the orator to encompass all the fields of wisdom, and wrote on many subjects, including law, religion, and moral philosophy. Since Cicero lived at a time when the great Greek and some of the Roman classical writers had already done their work, his books were a mine of information about many aspects of classical culture. Given these characteristics of ancient rhetoric, it is not surprising that the Renaissance humanists thought their celebration of classical oratory could contribute to a general revival of Roman and Greek culture. To a considerable degree, they were right.

The second reason for the humanist celebration of rhetoric emerge from the first: Rhetoric did not have the same purpose for them that it has come to have for us. The aim of rhetoric was not bombast or even primarily the creation of aesthetically pleasing speech, but eloquence, and eloquence meant persuasive power. An eloquent speech was one that not only taught its audience something and entertained or pleased its hearers, an eloquent speech *moved* its listeners, it persuaded them, it actually affected their lives. Thus Leonardo Bruni wrote that eloquence was necessary to men in their social life, in order to "win over the minds of others, break the power of evildoers, and recommend justice." It was eloquence that made human speech not only a means of communication, but an important influence on human action. By its force a social group might bring its own values into public view and reenforce its own commitment to them. Public orations often lasted for hours during the Renaissance, and were listened to with an enthusiasm that strikes the modern observer with awe. These speeches seem to have drawn their audience together and given them a sense of community much as the drama would in a slightly later period, or as folk singing does for many people today.

And the third reason is that the humanists themselves usually gave the speeches on such occasions. The best way to describe the occupation of the Renaissance humanists is to say that they were professional rhetoricians. This does not mean that they were primarily public speakers, although speaking in public was an important part of their activity. Rather, they were the professionally literate members of their society, often serving as secretaries to independent towns like Florence, or to ruling princes like the duke of Milan. The office of chancellor, held by some of the outstanding humanists, was essentially that of a secretary on the highest level. The chancellor was responsible for the records kept in deliberations of councils, and for the diplomatic correspondence of his town or prince with other governments. Much of the energy of humanists like Antonio Loschi in Milan and Coluccio Salutati in Florence went into writing official correspondence. Apart from that, many of the humanists were professional rhetoricians in that they taught rhetoric and allied subjects in the schools and universities. Both at Florence and at Venice, public instruction in rhetoric had a connection with the activity of the chancery.

As a professional group, the chancellors and rhetoricians of the fifteenth century were not a new element in Italian life; men with similar tasks and orientations had also existed in the medieval Italian towns at least from the thirteenth century on. But the genuinely classical character of humanist culture was new and original in the Renaissance. The reasons for the emergence of humanist culture within this traditional group are of course complex, but they may be briefly stated as follows. First, the evolution of Italy since the thirteenth century had transformed the main Italian centers from small towns dominated by guild organizations and each having limited influence outside its walls to territorial states with considerable power over the surrounding region and with a political organization that dwarfed the previously dominant great guilds. In this new situation, the old Greco-Roman ideal of the city-state had increasing relevance, and the culture produced by the ancients was more clearly and easily understood. Second, the medieval struggle between the German emperors and the popes for control of the Italian peninsula ended after 1300, as both the papacy and the empire entered a period of crisis in the fourteenth century. Italians no longer had to seek the meaning of their actions in some kind of relationship to these external powers, as Dante had done in his treatise *On Monarchy;* they were free to examine their public life in terms that were closer to their everyday experience. Third, the crisis of the papacy—its removal to Avignon at the beginning of the fourteenth century followed by the Great Schism in the Church after 1378—meant a crisis of values for thoughtful Europeans. The humanists were seldom tempted to try to replace Christianity with classical culture, but they often thought they could purify and enhance the spiritual life of their time by an infusion of classical ideals within a basically Christian framework.

These are some of the main reasons for the development of the program of classical culture embodied in the *studia humanitatis* as we have outlined it above. To fill in the outline somewhat, let us look at two important figures in Renaissance humanism, Petrarch or Francesco Petrarca (1304–74) and Lorenzo Valla (1407–54).

Petrarch is usually said to be the first humanist. He played a larger role than anyone else in making men conscious of the full and rich content of classical culture, and of the meaning of the ideal of eloquence. Petrarch's humanism is not as fully developed as that of some of his followers; his literary style and his understanding of the classics were still colored by medieval features that later humanists would discard. But the later evolution of humanism in the Renaissance is present in his thought as in an embryo: The characteristics of the later development can be discerned there in less clear shape and on a smaller scale. Moreover, despite the "impurity" of his style from a classical point of view and the presence of medieval features in his thought, Petrarch's personal stature is at least as great as that of any of his followers. Many people believe that he was not only the first but also the greatest humanist of the Italian Renaissance.

When people read Petrarch today they are likely to read the poetry he wrote in Italian, or more precisely, in Tuscan, since there was no fully common language in the Italy of his day. This is great poetry, presenting with charm and passion the inner history of a human love—Petrarch's own love for Laura. His greatness in this kind of poetry was recognized in the Renaissance. Yet what he himself probably hoped to be remembered for was not this Italian poetry but his many writings in Latin. Latin was the language of the learned world in the Middle Ages (the "Latin Quarter" of Paris is the part of the city where the students and teachers of the university lived), and the language of Petrarch's favorite authors, the poet Virgil and the orator Cicero. It was also the "official" language of Renaissance humanism. Later humanists would learn Greek and some even Hebrew, but they communicated among themselves in Latin. Petrarch wrote poetry in Latin, notably a long and never completed epic about the Roman general Scipio Africanus, *Africa*. Several of Petrarch's friends and disciples who read this poem were disappointed by it, and few people today believe that it is worthy of comparison with his Italian poetry. He also wrote many prose works in Latin. Among these were works of "history" (we would probably class them as biography) about the great men of the past, treatises on moral philosophy, and commentaries—often sharply polemical—on the intellectual problems of his day. In addition he wrote an impressive number of letters.

Petrarch's letters are worthy of our attention. He wrote to many different people on a wide variety of subjects, describing events and persons of the day, exhorting and reproving his correspondents, stating his attitude toward all kinds of questions. Petrarch kept copies of his letters, arranged them in a sequence (not always the same as the order in which he had written them), and polished their style and content in order to make a finished literary product out of them. There was a certain amount of artificiality, of posing in Petrarch's letters; he addressed his friends with classical names,

calling them "my Socrates," or "my Laelius" or "Olympius." Sometimes he embroidered his experiences so that it is hard to know
whether there is any kernel of truth in what he says. In one famous
example he wrote of climbing the highest mountain in Provence,
Mt. Ventoux; reaching the top after a long and difficult climb, he
opened his copy of St. Augustine's *Confessions* "by accident" to the
most appropriate passage (one berating men for being curious
about what is at the top of mountains instead of examining their
own inner life), then descended the mountain, returned to a nearby
village, and there wrote a fifteen-page letter in polished Latin
describing the experience—all in a single day. Whether Petrarch
actually climbed the mountain is unclear; if he did, he was more
interested in the allegorical moral he found in St. Augustine than
he was in the experience of the hike. Petrarch's posing is striking
too in his letter "To Posterity," telling later men who might have
heard of him what he wanted them to know about himself, and in
his letters to classical authors, telling Cicero, Seneca and Livy
what he thought of them. There is much in these letters that strikes
the modern reader as silly. Yet there is something very significant
about them too, for what Petrarch's posturings and artificiality
show is that he had a remarkable consciousness of his individuality
and his place in history. His intensely developed self-consciousness
was—to adopt the formula of a modern psychologist—both an
awareness of himself by himself, and an awareness of himself as
the object of other people's observation. Perhaps we can find some
of the sources of this self-consciousness in Petrarch's relation to
his time.

In his comments on the intellectual situation of his day, Petrarch
had harsh words to say about two groups of fourteenth-century
thinkers and writers: physicians and dialecticians. A twentieth-
century reader might expect that his hostility to physicians was
directed against medical *practice* in the fourteenth century, since
it seems likely that physicians then did as much harm to their pa-
tients as good. But Petrarch was not so much bothered by practicing
physicians as he was annoyed by medical theorists, and by the
kinds of intellectual activity carried on in the medical schools.
Fourteenth-century physicians were among the most enthusiastic
students of "natural philosophy" of the time, and their image of a
learned man was one who knew the contents of the available
treatises on biology and botany with their various commentaries.
Petrarch had two objections to these physicians and their culture.

One was their lack of training in or sympathy for literature, their failure to appreciate the stylistic excellence and the eloquence of Cicero and other classical writers. Like many scientists in other times and places, these physicians were not concerned about writing in a manner that would be pleasing or even comprehensible to men not trained in their subject, and they did not value these kinds of literary attainments in others. To Petrarch this meant that "only 'infantile inability to speak' and perplexed stammering 'wisdom' trying hard to keep one eye open and 'yawning drowsily,' as Cicero calls it, is held in good repute nowadays." Tied to this neglect of style and of communication was a second fault of the physicians: their passion for the details of natural philosophy to the exclusion— Petrarch thought—of a sufficient concern about human life and action. "What is the use—I beseech you—of knowing the nature of quadrupeds, fowls, fishes, and serpents and not knowing or even neglecting man's nature, the purpose for which we are born, and whence and whereto we travel?" In this criticism of the physicians there is a strong vein of religious concern, and Petrarch accused some of his opponents of being indifferent to Christianity. But his main concern was less about religious dogma than about right living, and his objection to the physicians was that their passion for delving into the secrets of nature turned them away from the more important task of improving men's lives. Instead of the natural science of the physicians, Petrarch recommended that men devote themselves to the study of ethics, of moral philosophy.

Given Petrarch's preference for a humanistic philosophy over a naturalistic science, it may be surprising to find him so critical of a second group of his contemporaries, the dialecticians or logicians. After all, dialectic or logic (Petrarch did not trouble to distinguish between the two) is an important component of most philosophy. Plato and Aristotle, both of whom Petrarch praised effusively, believed that logic was the starting point of philosophy, the foundation of philosophical wisdom. Why then did Petrarch attack dialecticians? Part of the reason may lie in the nature of the teachers of dialectic in his time, who seem to have taken great delight in logical disputations for their own sake, even when they did not believe that fundamental truths could come out of them. But this criticism, while it was repeated by many later humanists, is rejected by many modern scholars, who point out that some of the scholastic logicians the humanists condemned made genuine contributions to the advance of science. In any event the main impulse for Petrarch's lack of sympathy with dialecticians does not lie in their activities but in his conception of what "true" philosophy was. To Petrarch, genuine moral philosophy had the purpose of making men virtuous. In this kind of philosophy, definition and logical deduction were less important than grammatical clarity and rhetorical exhortation. Moral philosophy was tied to powerful speech, to eloquence. "The true moral philosophers and useful teachers of the virtues are those whose first and last intention is to make hearer and reader good, those who do not merely teach what virtue and vice are and hammer into our ears the brilliant name of the one and the grim name of the other but sow into our hearts love of the best and eager desire for it and at the same time hatred of the worst and how to flee it." It was not truth which Petrarch desired from moral philosophy, but goodness. "It is better to will the good than to know the truth."

But how was one to know what the good was? Logical inquiry was one answer, but Petrarch had little sympathy with it. Religion also provided a description of goodness, one which Petrarch admired and certainly never rejected. Yet Petrarch persistently refused to enter into the religious life as it was understood in his time — the life of monasticism. His brother became a monk and Petrarch hailed him for it, but that could not be his own way. Thus the good which Petrarch willed is less easily described than it would have been had he allowed logic or religion to define it. Basically, Petrarch accepted the notion of goodness which was implicit in the customs of his day and in the actions of eminent and respected men. He did not regard philosophical precepts as moral absolutes, but rather as reinforcement for a man's resolve to live as well as he could. He would have agreed with Cicero's dictum: "We should know the precepts of philosophy, but live according to the standards of civil society." As Petrarch wrote in a letter to a friend: "You will act differently as a philosopher than you do as a man. No one is so given to wisdom that he does not, when he returns to the common human state, conform also to the mores of civil society."

From a philosophic point of view, this is a weak and inconsistent position. What is the point of knowing ethical principles, if one is not going to live according to them? Petrarch answered this question in a work he called his *Secret*, or *On the Secret Conflict of My Cares*. What he said there was that human nature is weak and inconsistent, so that men are not able to live in accord with the

exalted visions of life worked out by reason. The *Secret* takes the
form of a dialogue between Petrarch and one of his spiritual and
intellectual mentors, St. Augustine, who berated Petrarch for his
immoderate attachment to worldly life, in particular for the energy
he gave to writing for a worldly audience instead of looking into
himself, and for the double fetters of his love for Laura and his
desire for glory that bound him to the present world. All these
attachments kept Petrarch from devoting himself wholeheartedly
to living in a way consistent with the great overarching final reality
of man's life: his death. Since the very definition of man must include his mortality, a rational ordering of human life must always
be mindful of the approach of death. This rather dreary message
had a Christian character in Petrarch's dialogue, but Petrarch did
not regard it as representing only a Christian point of view. After
all, it was the pagan philosopher Plato who had defined philosophy
as a preparation for death, and that idea had been repeated by
other non-Christian authors, notably Cicero and the Stoics. What
St. Augustine said was therefore not only in accord with Christian
teaching, it was also the point of view of human reason itself: man's
happiness depended on freeing himself from worldly, transient
concerns, and devoting himself to a life of reason and virtue. The
desire for literary fame, and the kind of passionate attachment
to a woman Petrarch displayed in his Italian poetry were not in
harmony with such a life. Petrarch's reaction to Augustine's message was ambivalent. Although he finally agreed to it with his
head he could not make Augustine's philosophical reason rule his
heart, or shape his life. He would continue to write, to seek fame,
and to love Laura. Human reason might show him that these were
not worthwhile concerns, but human nature could not allow him
to give them up. Petrarch could understand and even love the
exalted vision of life Augustine presented to him, but (as he wrote
elsewhere) "because of the frailties and burdens of mortal life,
which are not only difficult to bear, but difficult merely to enumer-
ate, I cannot, I confess, lift up, however ardently I should wish,
the inferior parts of my soul" to the level of that vision. This means
that Petrarch after his dialogue with St. Augustine would continue
to live pretty much as he had before. He would keep St. Augustine's
words continually before himself, in order to be reminded of what
his life might be like if he were a fully rational creature, and in
order to re-orient himself continually toward those values he recognized as the highest ones. But the final result would only be to

confirm him in a life of moderation, living as a man of flesh and blood, neither mired in vices nor capable of the purest virtues.

This meant that Petrarch accepted a life of contradiction: His actions could not conform to his values. Such a life is the life of common sense, of ordinary men like us who often find ourselves — to our dismay — saying one thing and doing another. Petrarch's humanism was in accord with the lives of the men of his time. His values were those of the men who comprised his audience. They, like him, understood the attractions of fame and love, and found themselves unable to act on the counsels of perfection that preachers and philosophers addressed to them. Yet it should be remembered that not all intellectuals simply reflect the values of their time: Many are highly critical of the life around them, and this was true in Petrarch's day as much as in ours. Why did Petrarch accept the values of common sense scorned by Plato and so many traditional philosophers? One reason lies in his closeness to the tradition of classical rhetoric and in his admiration for Cicero. The orator who wants to be effective cannot depart too far from the language and values of his audience. As a speaker in one of Cicero's dialogues put it: "Whereas in all other arts that is most excellent which is farthest removed from the understanding and mental capacity of the untrained, in oratory the very cardinal sin is to depart from the language of everyday life, and the usage approved by the sense of the community." Petrarch understood this tie between the orator and society, and his humanism was partially shaped by it. The importance of rhetoric in the *studia humanitatis* tied the humanists to the world of common sense.

Unlike Cicero, however, Petrarch was greatly troubled by his own acceptance of the limitations which kept him within the circle of ordinary life. He regarded it as a sign of human weakness, and his sense of men's inability to live up to their ideals dismayed him. Petrarch was altogether a melancholy and pessimistic man. In the *Secret* he described himself as afflicted with a disease called in Latin *accidia,* a kind of world-weariness, a dislike of everything about oneself, a dissatisfaction with the very state of being human. Coloring his pessimism is the fact that he lived in one of the dreariest and most depressing ages in history. The fourteenth century was a time of widespread disruption due to warfare and the crises in fundamental institutions like the Catholic Church. It was also the time of the worst outbreak of disease in European history: Coming in the middle of the century, the plague called the Black

Death carried off a third or more of the population in many areas, including several of Petrarch's close friends. Living in such an environment, Petrarch naturally doubted the ability of men to master their fate, and felt the uncertainty of his own existence. Perhaps the intense and nearly overpowering self-consciousness we found in his letters is an attempt to compensate for this doubt: By assuring himself that he was perceived by others, Petrarch may have strengthened the otherwise weak hold which a man of the fourteenth century had on human existence. In his humanism we find no glorification of man, no exalted sense of human possibilities. Instead Petrarch reminds us that man must always struggle to retain his hold on a truly human existence, to realize his highest capacities—and that this work is never done.

Lorenzo Valla was a different kind of man, who lived in a different sort of world. Yet his intellectual orientation was along the lines of Petrarch's, whose rhetorical humanism he developed to a much more advanced level. Personally he was the opposite of Petrarch: Extravagant and exultant where Petrarch had been brooding and restrained, Valla retained all through his life the characteristics of a precocious and disrespectful youth. This sometimes got him into trouble, even bringing on him a charge of heresy, but Valla's self-confidence was not shaken by the doubts of other people. These characteristics of Valla's personality seem representative of many aspects of the century in which he lived. The fifteenth century was one of recovery from the disruption and despair of the fourteenth, as well as a time of remarkable and self-conscious achievement in many fields. The humanist movement itself had made much progress since Petrarch's day. Petrarch had talked of imitating ancient writers, but his own style bore little resemblance to Cicero's. Valla and his contemporaries could write the Latin of the Romans, and in some cases were able to pass off their works as ancient products, to the confusion of later generations of scholars. Valla himself had a remarkably intimate knowledge of classical Latin, and he shared this knowledge with others in an immense treatise, "On the Elegances of the Latin Language." Here he discussed the proper usage of a host of difficult words, carefully explaining the subtle differences between related words and phrases, seeking to reverse the evolution that had taken place in the Latin language in the Middle Ages and to equate it once again unconditionally with Roman literary practice.

Some critics of the humanists have attacked Valla for his linguistic purism: Through such activities, they say, the humanists killed Latin, changing it from the living, evolving language it had been in the Middle Ages into a dead relic unrelated to real life. Such criticism contains an important truth. But Valla's linguistic studies were not simply an expression of purist intellectual elitism. Behind them was a drive to uncover the historical reality of the ancient world, to distinguish the classical past from what had followed it. In this the humanists largely succeeded, and their success is well illustrated by another of Valla's works, his "Oration on the False Donation of Constantine." The so-called Donation of Constantine is a document which played an important role in medieval history, since it purported to be the deed by which Emperor Constantine conveyed in the fourth century important secular powers to the pope as head of the Roman Church. In fact it was an early medieval forgery. Several writers attacked the forged Donation during the Middle Ages, and Valla was not the first to deny its authenticity. But he was the first to see it for what it was: a medieval construction whose language betrayed it as a product of the post-classical, not the classical age. Earlier critics of the Donation had regarded its author as a villain, but to Valla he was a fool. One of his blunders had been to speak of Satraps as part of Constantine's court. Valla knew that there had been no Satraps in Constantine's court (in fact they were officers of the *Persian* Empire) and reviled the author of the forgery: "Numbskull! Blockhead! What have Satraps to do with the matter?" Valla could distinguish—as medieval men usually could not—between what was authentically ancient and what only pretended to be.

Valla had a lively enthusiasm for antiquity, but his attitude toward ancient thinkers was by no means uncritical. Like other men, he approached ancient culture in the pursuit of his own purposes. What these purposes were can perhaps best be seen in Valla's main discussion of moral philosophy, a dialogue he called (in its different versions) *On Pleasure* or *On the True Good*. This work was modeled on classical dialogues, notably those of Cicero, and its discussion proceeded by way of several set speeches. The subject was human happiness: What made man happy, and what was therefore "good" for man? Valla found three different answers in classical philosophy, each one deriving from a different philosophical school: the Stoics, the Peripatetics, and the Epicureans. The Stoics were the most rigorous and most "philosophical" of the

three. They taught that the happy man was the same as the wise
man, and that this wise man cared for only one thing: virtue or
moral worth. Only virtue was firm and stable, unaffected by the
storms of life, and only by clinging to virtue alone could man
achieve uninterrupted happiness. Only virtue was wholly good;
other things might be desirable, like health and riches, but since
an evil man could turn them to evil ends, they were not worthy of
being called "good," nor of being the object of man's quest. They
could not make the wise man happy. The Peripatetics (Aristotle
was one) took a more moderate position. They agreed with the
Stoics that virtue was superior to any other goal man could set for
himself, and that no man who was not virtuous was happy. But
they thought the Stoic philosophy too rigid, and not based on a
real understanding of human nature. Man was not a disembodied
spirit, but a composite being of soul and flesh at once. His happiness had to take account of this. Therefore the Peripatetics concluded that human happiness was based first of all on virtue, but
that it had to include good health and external circumstances—a
moderate degree of wealth, for instance—too. The Epicureans
differed from both. What really made man happy, they believed,
was pleasure. In saying this they did not mean to encourage an
undisciplined hedonism; on the contrary, the ideal of conduct of
the ancient Epicureans was quite chaste. As Cicero pointed out
(and he was Valla's major source in these matters), Epicurus had
denied that any man could take pleasure in a life that was not
lived with justice and morality. But what made such a life happy
was the pleasure it gave, not the virtue it contained. It followed
that the man in search of happiness should avoid any activity that
might cause him pain—even if "duty" called him to it. Of the three
schools, the Epicureans were not the least virtuous, but they were
the least responsive to claims originating outside the individual.

As already noted, this three-headed approach to moral philosophy derived from Cicero. In presenting it Cicero did not always
take the same side. In some places he favored the Stoics, but in
others he favored the Peripatetics. The one school that did not
attract him was the Epicureans. However chastely one sought to
define it, their advocacy of a life based on pleasure seemed repre-
hensible to a Roman statesman with a strong sense of duty. Petrarch had followed Cicero in this, sometimes presenting a Stoic
view of ethics, sometimes the more moderate Peripatetic one, but
never praising the Epicureans. When it came to be Valla's turn
to discuss these questions, however, he refused to follow Cicero

and Petrarch. In frank and conscious opposition to them (and to most writers in his own times) he chose the Epicureans. Pleasure was the true good for man, the source of human happiness.

Valla's advocacy of the Epicureans has often fascinated students of the Renaissance. It seems to support the idea that the fifteenth century was a time of libertinism and immorality. Valla's presentation of the Epicurean point of view had little of the restraint of classical writers. His vibrant rejection of all that interfered with pleasure reached its height in an imagined speech of a vestal virgin on the pains and horrors of chastity. Yet this is not the whole story, for the final judgment in favor of Epicureanism in the dialogue is not given by a libertine, but by a pious Christian. Moreover, the grounds of the Christian preference for the Epicureans were clearly serious. Stoicism was fundamentally anti-Christian, the argument ran, because it pretended that man could find happiness through human virtue, that is by himself, without the intervention of Christ. From a Christian point of view this was clearly unacceptable. Christianity taught that virtue was *not* its own reward, but that man should follow virtue because it would lead him to a higher end, an end that Epicurus had quite properly identified with pleasure, and which Christianity recognized as the pleasure of the heavenly life. Thus Epicureanism contained a view of human nature which harmonized quite easily with Christian belief, whereas the other philosophical schools—especially the Stoics—attributed too much to man to leave any place in life for God.

If Valla's purpose in writing this treatise was to veil his own real beliefs and to confuse subsequent generations of historians, he certainly succeeded. Most readers of Valla's dialogue find either insincerity or ambiguity at the center of it. Yet Valla's purpose was not to bewilder his readers. A careful consideration of the work can dispel this uncertainty, and show that his aim was clear and comprehensible, if only we are willing to understand it in his own terms. In the preface, Valla explained his reason for writing this dialogue. It was, he said, to discredit philosophy and philosophers. Now, Petrarch had written against philosophers too: against the logicians and natural philosophers of the medieval schools. But Valla's purpose was much larger. It was not medieval philosophy he wanted to attack, but ancient philosophy as well. His strategy was to set the philosophers against one another, and to demonstrate that the ones usually thought to be the worst—the Epicureans—were superior to the best and most "philosophical"—the Stoics. Certainly this is what he did in the treatise. Still, it seems hard at first to take Valla's declaration of his purpose seriously, because we cannot imagine that anyone so enthusiastic about antiquity would seriously write against its thinkers. The key to resolving this dilemma is the recognition that what evoked Valla's enthusiasm was not ancient culture in general, but ancient literary and rhetorical culture—the works of the orators, poets and historians, not the writings of the philosophers. Valla opposed ancient philosophical culture, as represented by Aristotle or even by Socrates. Like the other votaries of the *studia humanitatis*, Valla saw himself primarily as an orator, and his ideal of the intellectual life was shaped by the study of rhetoric. His understanding of what this involved was more extravagant and uncompromising than that of other humanists, just as his whole personality was more flamboyant than theirs. Whereas other humanists, Petrarch and Leonardo Bruni, for instance, had sought to ennoble rhetoric by uniting it with philosophy, Valla sought to exalt oratory by subordinating philosophy to it. "Philosophy is like a soldier or a tribune under the command of oratory, the queen," he wrote. Thus there is nothing paradoxical about Valla's expressed desire to discredit ancient philosophy in *On Pleasure;* it is consistent with his general orientation, and with his personality.

Understanding this also allows us to interpret Valla's moral position in the dialogue. Valla was not a libertine, and he was not conducting a frontal attack on all morality. What he abhorred was the idea that *philosophy* could determine the proper standards of human behavior. It is in opposition to ancient *philosophical* morality that the people in Valla's dialogue oppose "virtue." But philosophy was not the only source of moral standards. Valla knew two others, both of which he accepted as legitimate. Of these, the first was Christianity. Valla was not anti-Christian. His attack on the Donation of Constantine was also an attack on the worldliness and corruption of the papacy, and some of his arguments in exposing the forgery were similar to the themes of contemporary religious reformers. Valla's Christianity was closer to that of ordinary laymen in the fifteenth century than it was to the religious conceptions of the clergy; it was also at times the somewhat casual Christianity of a society whose fundamental religious unity had yet to be seriously challenged. But since this was the Christianity of many people in Valla's day, we cannot single him out as irreligious because of it: He was a loyal Christian and accepted the right of the Church to direct men's lives. Valla's second source of moral standards is already familiar to us from Petrarch: It was common sense, the standards of respected men in everyday life. Valla's writings are full of assertions of the superiority of common sense to the abstractions of philosophers. Just as in linguistic matters Valla upheld the standard of common usage in opposition to the innovative "rigor" of philosophical language, so in ethics he believed that ordinary behavior was a better guide than the speculations of the philosophers. Valla's morality was therefore the morality of average Christian men in his day. In such a morality, pleasure was certainly important, but the pursuit of it was limited by the need to carry on social life, business and politics.

To say that Valla's ethical standards were based on common sense is to say that his ethical position was that of an orator. Valla, like Cicero and Petrarch, recognized the orator's close tie to his audience, and he accepted — even gloried in — the intellectual and moral limitations this imposed. But Valla took this rhetorical emphasis on custom and everyday life into a new area, for he argued that rhetoric — not philosophy, as the medieval scholastics had thought — was the intellectual discipline that could come closest to Christian belief. The orator was able to agree with the Christian because both denied that men could rise above the mediocre level of common human existence either by their own efforts or in the present life. Philosophers might try to work out new standards of conduct or utopian conceptions of existence (like that in Plato's *Republic*, for instance) and tell men that they could find happiness in such ways; in doing so they would be claiming too much for the power of unaided human reason. The orator, on the other hand, firm in his acceptance of the limitations of ordinary human life, saw that these limitations could be transcended only by the action of God, not of men, and in the next life rather than the present one. Thus the eloquence of the orator could aid in the spread of the Christian message, whereas the reason of philosophers was the source of many heresies.

What was new and original in Valla's thinking in this regard was not his conception of religion, but his view of how religion was related to intellectual life. In the Middle Ages, the dominant view had been that theology could be aided by philosophy, since philosophy, like religion, was committed to truth. Rhetoric was often suspect because it might be employed to urge falsehood rather than truth; the techniques of eloquence were used by preachers, but theologians were trained in logic rather than rhetoric. With

Valla this relationship between the various intellectual disciplines began to change, and the change would have important consequences. In the sixteenth century, the humanist Erasmus would use many of Valla's ideas and techniques to work toward a new concept of theology in which exhortation was more important than speculation, and conduct more important than abstract truth. Like Valla, Erasmus upheld a notion of intellectual life in which grammar and rhetoric were the formative disciplines, rather than logic or dialectic. Erasmus was opposed by the same kind of people who opposed Valla: the teachers of traditional philosophy and theology in the universities and in the schools of the religious orders. It was members of this same group who brought charges of heresy against Valla. What troubled and threatened them was not any particular doctrinal position he took, but his general conception of intellectual life in which rhetoric was superior to philosophy, and common sense to elaborate speculation.

If Petrarch's humanism was a reminder that man must always struggle to maintain and fulfill his humanity, Valla's was a much more confident affirmation of man as he is in his ordinary social life. Valla was in many ways the most extreme and uncompromising of all the representatives of the *studia humanitatis;* for that reason he reveals some of the underlying characteristics of the whole movement more clearly than other humanists do. In particular he demonstrates the prime historical paradox of Renaissance humanism, namely that it was deeply conservative and profoundly radical at the same time. It was conservative in its acceptance and glorification of custom and common sense, and in its resistance to rational criticism of day-to-day thinking. Thus Renaissance humanism is strikingly different from the later humanism of the Enlightenment and the nineteenth century (and even from some currents of sixteenth-century thought), whose energizing principle was the ability of man to remake his own world through reason. The philosophers of the eighteenth century announced their purpose as *changer la façon commune de penser,* "to change the ordinary way of thinking." The aim of Renaissance humanists was the opposite, to recall thought to the ways of ordinary men, to establish common sense as the high court of the world of the mind. To do so was to place a tight rein on the rational imagination, to clip the wings of thought before it could take off on any philosophic flight. But in the world of the declining Middle Ages, this deeply conservative program had a radical cutting edge. At this time the dominant thinkers and those most bound to tradition were philosophers and theologians whose views of morality and thought were often unsympathetic to everyday life and common sense. The fundamental distinction in the Catholic church between the clergy and the laity militated against the idea that the life of ordinary men might be a source of enlightenment about fundamental values, and the whole elaborate medieval tradition of hierarchy in every sector of society and every branch of learning argued against the notion that "lower" things—whether men or their activities— could make laws for "higher" ones. By the fifteenth century this hierarchical structure of institutions and beliefs weighed heavily on many sensitive men, and the humanist emphasis on common sense fit well with many of the themes of contemporary religious reformers, for whom the distinction between the morality of laymen and some supposedly "higher" morality made little sense. Thus the concerns of the humanists point toward the profound historical changes that would come with the Reformation. However conservative the defense of custom and common sense would come to seem later, in the fifteenth century this theme could have a clearly radical import.

There is no abstract and eternal humanism, valid in all times and places. There are only men, living in a world not entirely of their making, and struggling to endow that world with human significance, to change it from an outside power in control of their lives to a product of their own humanity over which men can exercise control. The humanists of the fifteenth century would not have stated their purpose in these terms, but this was still their aim: to make their world more human, to recall men to themselves.

BIBLIOGRAPHICAL NOTE: For a more fully worked out version of the interpretation of Renaissance humanism given here, see J. E. Seigel, *Rhetoric and Philosophy in Renaissance Humanism* (Princeton, 1968). This interpretation borrows a great deal from the work of Paul O. Kristeller, *Renaissance Thought* (New York, 1961). For a different approach to the subject, see Hans Baron, *The Crisis of the Early Italian Renaissance* (2nd ed., Princeton, 1966). A good selection of humanist texts in English is *The Renaissance Philosophy of Man*, ed. E. Cassirer, P. O. Kristeller and J. H. Randall (Chicago, 1948). There is a translation of Petrarch's

Secret by Wm. H. Draper (London, 1911). Petrarch's self-consciousness is illuminated by the work of R. D. Laing; see *The Divided Self* (Penguin ed., Baltimore, 1965), Chapter 7. There is no available English version of Valla's *De voluptate*. There is an Italian translation in L. Valla, *Scritti filosofici e religiosi,* ed., Giorgio Radetti, (Florence, 1953).

PRINTING AND THE SPREAD OF HUMANISM IN GERMANY: THE EXAMPLE OF ALBRECHT VON EYB
❧ Rudolf Hirsch

Some thirty years ago the

late Professor George Sarton, the well-known historian of science, wrote: "The general spirit of the [early] printers was retrograde rather than progressive; most of their novelties were 'curiosities' in the vulgar sense rather than glorious adventures of the human spirit." I disagree with Dr. Sarton. Printers were literate carftsmen or businessmen who produced primarily what they believed to be in demand. Their production reflected the taste of the actual or presumed reading public and only very secondarily their own taste, preference or predilection. Ambitious printers who assessed the market shrewdly tended to favor a balanced program which would include novel as well as traditional texts. Up to the last decade of the fifteenth century there was rarely an important and successful printer who committed himself to a uniform specialized program.

The art of printing with movable type was invented between the late 1430s and the early 1450s by Johann Gutenberg in Strasbourg and Mainz. Within two generations after its perfection printing had spread to over 250 towns in various parts of Europe and had affected not only the dissemination of ideas but also, used as an instrument of information and propaganda, historical events. Church and secular governments adopted the new medium almost immediately, and made it serve their purposes. Books, pamphlets, and broadsides were issued to criticize, or malign, traditional concepts and to promote new ones. Printed books were used in formal and informal education with the inevitable result that more and more men, women and children learned to read. It was only natural that the new art or craft influenced the lives of many in large parts of Europe. Through printing it was possible to produce hundreds of copies in the same time that it had taken formerly to copy a single text by hand. During the fifteenth century alone an estimated 40,000 titles were published. Counting an average of 250 copies per title, which is probably a low estimate, the presses produced during a period of approximately fifty years the staggering total of at least 10 million items. It is further suggested that by the year 1517, the year when Luther's *Ninety-five Theses* were posted, perhaps another 10 million items were issued. Soon thereafter propaganda publications for and against the Reformation literally flooded the market, and it is a fair guess that by the middle of the sixteenth century no fewer than 150,000 titles had been produced in more than 60 million copies. The age of the singly handmade book was indeed drawing to an end, and the age of the mass-produced book had begun.

The Reformation, the German Peasant Revolt of 1525, the consolidation of royal power in France and England, or the rise of capitalism might well have taken a different course had printing not been invented. Without the presses, how quickly, or rather how slowly, would new achievements and ideas in the sciences—like those of the mathematicians and astronomers Regiomontanus or Copernicus, the botanists Fuchs or Brunfels, or the medical innovators Vesalius and Paracelsus—have become known, subsequently to be accepted, criticized or rejected? Would humanism have succeeded as well as it did without the many printed texts that served to disseminate new ideas, along with a knowledge of the classics, throughout civilized Europe? It is this latter question which I shall try to answer in this essay.

Humanism spread to German lands before the invention of printing. The chancellor of Emperor Charles IV in Prague, Johann von Neumarkt (d. 1380), had exchanged letters with the arch-humanist Petrarch, and so had the emperor. The political adventurer and friend of Petrarch, Cola di Rienzo, had been in Bohemia from 1350 to 1352 and had exchanged views with influential men connected with the imperial court. Many more Italian humanists

came north during the first half of the fifteenth century, especially
during the councils of Constance (1414–1417) and Basel (1431–
1449), where they consorted with learned colleagues from transalpine countries, traveling in their spare time in search of classical
manuscripts. In 1442 Aeneas Sylvius Piccolomini (the later Pope
Pius II) joined the chancellery of Emperor Frederick III and during
his stay in Germany he promoted humanist ideals, and the improved style of Latin rhetoric and writing in imitation of Cicero.
In spite of these and similar contacts the influence of Italian humanism on German scholars remained quite limited until the latter
part of the fifteenth century.

Understandably then the earliest printers did not immediately
turn to the production of classical and humanist texts. Instead they
selected texts which were known to them to have been in steady
demand during the late manuscript period; these were primarily
sacred and liturgical texts, collections of sermons, theological disputations, devotional literature, law codes and commentaries,
school books, calendars and indulgences. But by 1465, two separate presses in different localities, Johann Furst and Peter Schoeffer
in Mainz and Ulrich Zell in Cologne, produced, quite independently
of each other, Cicero's *De officiis.* This was the first printing of a
classical work. The edition of Mainz, which also included Cicero's
Paradoxa, was apparently a commercial success, or Furst and
Schoeffer would not have reprinted it so soon thereafter in 1466;
by then the original edition of 1465 must have been sold out, or
nearly so.

In 1465 another important event took place. Printing was brought
to Italy (specifically to Subiaco near Rome) by two Germans, Conrad Sweynheim and Arnold Pannartz. The production of classical
and humanist volumes began to flourish in Italy almost at once.
Eight classical authors (Cicero, Apuleius, Gellius, Caesar, Lucanus,
Pliny, Virgil and Livy) had been published there by the end of
1469, while German printers at home still had only Cicero to their
credit. No wonder that Victor Scholderer of the British Museum,
one of this century's outstanding authorities on early printing,
concluded that "Italy stands out intellectually well ahead of the
rest of western Europe. There is no subject in which she is not to
the fore . . . and there are several, notably the humanities and
natural sciences in which she had something of a monopoly, so that
students in other countries were highly dependent upon her presses
for their means of instruction."

Excellent as Mr. Scholderer's characterization is, his claim that Italy was "intellectually well ahead" requires some modification or explanation. The very fact that Italy in general, and Venice in particular, exported classical and humanist texts to countries beyond the Alps in considerable number leads not only to the realization that the sales organization there was superior to that of any other country, but also shows that there were readers in the north who were important customers for exactly the type of publication which, characterized as progressive, gave Italy an unchallenged lead until the first half of the sixteenth century. Indeed classical and humanist texts found their way to Germany in considerable number. Specific instances of importation have been recorded in many places. The Nuremberg humanist Hartmann Schedel, for example, purchased in or about the year 1471 texts of Apuleius, Caesar, Cicero, Gellius, Livy, Strabo and Virgil; all these produced by Sweynheim and Pannartz in Rome. Let it also be noted that the most effective combine organized for the sale of printed books in Italy during the 1470s and 1480s was formed by Frenchmen, and primarily Germans in Venice (Nicolaus Jenson, Jacques LeRouge, Johann Rauchfass, Peter Ugelheimer, Caspar von Dinslaken, etc.), and that a multitude of Italian presses producing classical and humanist texts were operated by German masters and journeymen.

As a final, but important modification of Mr. Scholderer's statement we may add that the production of texts serving new learning was not quite as much of an Italian monopoly as is generally stated. For example, the first printed edition of Terence's comedies appeared in Strasbourg about the year 1470. It was produced by Johann Mentelin, who is much better known as the printer of Bibles, of works by St. Augustine, and of Wolfram von Eschenbach's famous epics *Parcival* and *Titurel.* The first printed edition of a single dialogue by the readable and entertaining Hellenistic satirist Lucian, his *The Ass,* was published by a little-known printer named Ludwig Hohenwang in Augsburg about the year 1477 in the Latin translation of Poggio Bracciolini. More importantly, the same printer concurrently issued a German edition, translated by Nikolaus von Wyle, which was the earliest printed vernacular rendering of a work by Lucian in any language. *The Ass* was the sole classical text printed by Hohenwang. The selection of this title was commercially sound, judging by the scarcity of both editions; they were apparently avidly read, or literally read

to pieces. Our last example is the most illuminating: The first col-
lected edition of Petrarch was not published in Italy, as one might
surmise, but in Basel in 1496. Available evidence clearly indicates
that the Latin writings of Petrarch were considerably more popular
in the north than in Italy. The printer of his *Opera* was a devotee
of humanism, Johann Amerbach.

These few examples can be multiplied many times to show that
while the contribution of German presses to the spread of classical
and humanist learning did not compare in the fifteenth century
with the Italian production, it was (like that of France and the
Low Countries) by no means negligible. Thus we note that texts
by the following authors were produced in Germany between
1465 and 1500:

CLASSICS

Cicero	Ovid	Sallust
Hesiod	Persius	Seneca
Horace	Phalarus	Tacitus
Isocrates	Plato	Terence
Juvenal	Plutarch	Tibullus
Lucian	Propertius	Virgil

—not to forget the ever-present
Aristotle.

HUMANISTS

Aeneas Sylvius	Francesco Filelfo
Leonardo Aretino	Giovanni Maria Filelfo
Baptista Mantuanus	Battista Guarino
Gasparino Barzizio	Antonio Mancinelli
Filippo Beroaldo	Petrarch
Giovanni Boccaccio	Poggio Bracciolini
Agostino Dati	Lorenzo Valla
Marsiglio Ficino	

Proper study and interpretation of the publishing history of
texts promoting new learning leads to a somewhat revised picture
of the cultural interaction between north and south. The presence
of Italians on German soil has been mentioned, but we might add
here that, beginning about the year 1480, Italian printer-publishers
began to attend the Frankfurt book fair to transact business and

also presumably to exchange information with their northern colleagues. To turn to the visits or prolonged stays of northerners
in Italy, we know that they were indeed frequent throughout the
fifteenth century. The matriculation records of Italian universities
that survived and have been published list hundreds of German
students. While law and medicine attracted more students than the
liberal arts, German scholars, even when studying for a professional career, came in contact with academics and townspeople
who were already imbued with a new, somewhat more questioning
attitude toward knowledge and learning. The intellectual climate
in fifteenth-century Italy reflected a novel enthusiasm for the
classics, for Latin rhetoric and style, for Roman law (as contrasted
with canon law) and law reform, and it was given to increased
creative and independent analyses that decreased dependence
upon traditional authorities. When German students returned
home, they often carried with them not only new ideas about religion, literature and the arts, but frequently classical and humanist
manuscripts, or later printed editions as well.

When we examine the membership of the Foundation of German
Merchants in Venice (the *Fondaco dei tedeschi*) we find among
the names those of patricians whose families played, or were to
play, important roles in the development of German humanism.
Attention may be drawn to Martin Behaim, geographer and astronomer, and Lorenz Behaim, lawyer and humanist, friend of
Johannes Reuchlin; Willibald Pirckheimer, friend and supporter
of Albrecht Dürer, and again a friend of Reuchlin; Hermann and
Hartmann Schedel, physicians and humanists in Nuremberg;
Marcus Welser, important humanist and antiquarian in the later
sixteenth century; Konrad Peutinger of Augsburg, adviser to
Emperor Maximilian I, and also a supporter of Reuchlin. Financial
or commercial connections between Italian and German centers
of trade were at times close and they also served, beyond economic
interest, the flow of ideas. German priests and monks flocked to
Italy. Lawyers, physicians, civil servants, artists, engineers and
soldiers—in other words men of all professions and representatives
of many trades—sojourned in Italy. Some of these returned dis-
enchanted, critical of the luxury and abuse which they had observed, especially at the Roman Curia. Others were impressed by
the elegance of the courts and stimulated by the intellectual activities; they went home with new, and at times fertile ideas.

Among tradesmen and craftsmen who went from German-speak-

ing lands to Italy were countless printers. They began their trek in
1465 (or slightly earlier), responding to the principle of supply
and demand. By then more persons had been trained in type found-
ing, typesetting and press work (i.e., the components of printing)
in Germany than could earn an adequate living at home. Conditions abroad, by contrast, were favorable. German printers established the first presses in Italy, France, Spain, Portugal, Hungary,
Bohemia, Moravia, Poland, Denmark and Sweden. Beyond Germany the demand for skilled printers existed and grew, while the
supply of native talent was sparse during the early period of printing. It is not surprising, therefore, that German masters and
journeymen alike came to Italy, where the many competing city
republics offered ample opportunities for work and sometimes
also financial backing and special privileges like freedom from
tolls and other duties, protection, or housing. Soon they were to
be found in practically every self-respecting Italian town, from
Naples in the south to Trento in the north, and from Cividale and
Udine in the east to Savigliano in the west. The proverbial *Wander-
lust* and *Drang nach dem Süden* also played their part, but primarily it was opportunity which beckoned. Not all of these men succeeded, and many went from town to town and from one failure
to another. Of those who returned home, some were impoverished,
others had money in their pockets; many brought along copies of
printed books that served later as models for new editions, or were
simply converted into cash or kind.

Throughout the manuscript period the selling of books was
active, but dealt with a limited volume of business. Thanks to
printing the amount of available merchandise increased greatly
and helped to make bookselling a profitable enterprise. The result
was a greatly expanded system of the book trade, which made it
possible for anybody who had the means to obtain classical and
humanist texts in nearby larger towns or, if not available there,
from Italy. Johannes Reuchlin, outstanding Hebrew scholar and
humanist and the center of the storm which became famous
through the publication of the *Letters of Obscure Men (Epistolae
obscurorum virorum)*, could write in 1502: "It is easy for me to
obtain from our own booksellers Latin books at moderate prices."
He still had to order Greek texts from Italy.

Some German scholars adopted humanism in its undiluted Italian form, like Peter Luder or Samuel Karoch. Few of their writings
are read or even known today. Within this group Conrad Celtis,
the first German poet laureate, is a notable exception; his name

is mentioned even today in the average textbook. To be truly effective and to exert a lasting influence transalpine humanism had to develop its own characteristics by combining national tradition with elements of the Italian Renaissance. In Germany mysticism, late scholasticism, and the deep concern with personal piety (as opposed to formal, organized religion) merged with the new interest in classical learning to create the admixture which is well described by the term Christian humanism. The concern with men's salvation and the reform of the church was more widespread among German than among Italian humanists. This may help to explain why so many Italian humanists seem oblivious of the common man, while the less polished and often less erudite German humanists tried in many cases to reach a wide circle, including even those men and women who could not read Latin. It was for them, at least in part, that a surprisingly large number of classical and humanist texts were translated, edited and printed within less than two generations after the first printing of Cicero (in 1465). I present here the names of classical and humanist authors printed in German translations up to the year 1520:

CLASSICS

Aesop	Cicero	Plutarch
Appolonius of Tyre	Galen	Sallust
Apuleius	Isocrates	Seneca
Aristotle	Livy	Terence
Avianus	Lucian	Valerius Maximus
Boethius	Ovid	Vegetius
Caesar	Plautus	Virgil
Cato	Pliny	

HUMANISTS

Aeneas Sylvius	Marsiglio Ficino
Baptista Mantuanus	Petrarch
Gasparino Barzizio	Giov. Pico della Mirandola
Giovanni Boccaccio	Poggio Bracciolini
Leonardo Bruni	Lorenzo Valla

Included in the list are only those authors whose individual or complete works were printed in full; extracts like those described on the following pages are excluded.

The case of one particular early humanist, Albrecht von Eyb, serves well to illustrate the special character of German humanism and its diffusion through the medium of printing. Albrecht von Eyb was born in 1420, a member of a well-to-do Franconian family which belonged to the lower nobility. He went to school in Erfurt and Rothenburg before leaving for Italy in 1444. There he entered the University of Pavia, first enrolling in the faculty of liberal arts. With some interruption he studied also in Bologna (1448, 1450–51, 1453) and Padua (1449). After an extended stay in Germany he received his doctorate in law in Pavia in 1459. In spite of his major in law he devoted a good deal of time and effort to the humanities. His own compilations during his stay in Italy and his later writings are the chief source of information on his scholarly activities and interests. From them we learn, for example, of his debt to his teacher of rhetoric Baldasare Rasino, and to Giovanni Lamola, whose *Praise of Chastity* strongly influenced Albrecht's own *Book of Marriage*. His background and training served him well in Germany where he occupied a number of important positions as cleric and jurisprudent. Pius II (Aeneas Sylvius) made Eyb papal chamberlain in 1458. He died in 1475 at a time when humanism and printing had become firmly rooted, but had not yet come to full fruition in Germany.

During his stay in Italy Albrecht von Eyb purchased manuscripts of classical and humanist authors, among them the comedies of Terence (copied from an older manuscript by another student at Bologna), the *Memorable Facts and Sayings* of Valerius Maximus, various works of Cicero, the writings of Poggio Bracciolini and Ugolino Pisani. He compiled his own manuscripts, filling them with complete texts or more often with sections and extracts from a great variety of authors then in vogue with Italian humanists. Fortunately many of these manuscripts have survived either in originals or in copies prepared in Germany by Hartmann Schedel. It is from his own library that Albrecht von Eyb culled the many stories which fill his major writings, describing the virtues and vices of men, the former to exhort men to strive for an honest and good life, the latter to learn to avoid pitfalls.

Albrecht von Eyb was not a brilliant man of letters, but he was very well read, a fair stylist and an intelligent interpreter. He cannot and should not be compared with the outstanding Italian humanists who were his contemporaries. But while the writings of a Poggio or Filelfo were applauded and praised by the Italian intelligentsia, Albrecht von Eyb's writings (and those of some other early humanists) had a broader impact on readers in Germany. Their influence was due in part to their popular form and their wide dissemination by the printing presses, as we shall see from a closer look at his two major compilations, the Latin *Margarita poetica* and the German *Ob einem Mann sei zu nehmen ein ehelich Weib oder nicht* ("Whether man should marry or not," hereafter quoted as *Book of Marriage,* or *Ehebuch*). The title of the *Margarita poetica,* written about the year 1459, means in literal translation *Pearl of Poetry,* but since Eyb uses the term poetic as an equivalent for humanist, it is also referred to here as the *Pearl of Humanism.* A handbook of rhetoric and letter writing, it is the first substantial book of this type composed by a German author. To illustrate the art of speaking and writing Albrecht von Eyb made a surprisingly wide selection from classical and humanist authors; a more or less complete list reads:

CLASSICS

Aesop	Juvenal	Prudentius
Apuleius	Macrobius	Seneca
Avianus	Martial	Statius
Caesar	Ovid	Terence
Cicero	Persius	Tibullus
Curtius Rufus	Plautus	Valerius Maximus
Diogenes Laertius	Plutarch	Virgil
		Vitruvius

HUMANISTS

Barzizio	Lamola
Battista di San Pietro	the anonymous Marrasius Elegy
Bessarion	Pamphilus Poem
Beccadelli	Petrarch
Botti	Poggio
Bruni	Rasino
Filelfo	Sacco
Guarino da Verona	

The careful reader of the *Margarita* thus acquired painlessly a broad knowledge of works which at that time were otherwise not easily available to Germans.

The *Pearl of Humanism* did not circulate widely in manuscript, but once it was printed in 1472 in Nuremberg by Johann Sensenschmidt it achieved considerable popularity. It was reprinted eleven times and produced four more times in abbreviated versions. In detail its printing history looks as follows:

4 editions produced in Strasbourg (not after 1479; 1483/4; not after 1485 — this edition possibly not printed in Strasbourg, but in Cologne; 1503)

2 editions produced in Basel (1495; 1503)

1 edition produced in Nuremberg (1472)

1 edition produced in an unidentified place in Germany (1502) (Early printed books often appeared without title, and without indication of place of printing, name of printer, or date.)

To these German editions are to be added:

2 editions produced in Rome (1475; 1480)

2 editions produced in Venice, possibly for export to Germany (1487; 1493)

3 abbreviated versions produced in Paris (between 1476 and 1478)

1 abbreviated edition produced in Toulouse (1492)

As stated earlier printers of the fifteenth century rarely developed a clearly progressive program. Of the eight editions produced in the German-speaking area only two editions, those printed in Basel, were the product of a printer committed to a classical and humanist program, Johann Amerbach. The other producers of Eyb's *Pearl of Humanism* favored a balanced program (J. Sensenschmidt in Nuremberg; G. Husner, the anonymous printer of the *Vitae Patrum*, and J. Prüss in Strasbourg). Not love of new learning but business acumen made them add the *Margarita* to their repertory.

From available evidence we estimate that the "average" edition of the *Margarita* was at least five hundred copies. The total number of copies for the eight editions printed in the German area thus amounted to four thousand, and presumably they were read by even more people. The success of the book is definitely established also by the fact that one astute man alone, the printer, publisher and bookseller Anton Koberger in Nuremberg, acquired one thousand six hundred copies of the two Basel editions for his sales organization. Notice that these two editions (1495 and 1503) therefore averaged more than eight hundred copies each. Around the year 1500, when literacy was still a limited achievement among broad classes of the population, the sale of several thousand copies of one title made it practically a bestseller. The last edition of the *Pearl* seems to have been issued in 1503. By then or soon thereafter the writings of many authors used by Albrecht von Eyb had become available in separate editions, and the new rhetoric (in imitation of the classics) had become an accepted standard for ambitious scholars and politicians alike. But not only these groups were to be influenced by the classical style. In the epilogue of the *Margarita* Albrecht von Eyb criticized the quasi-mechanical sermonizing from the pulpits and expressed his hope that improved rhetoric would also improve the quality and effectiveness of the preachers of the Gospel, a proposition stated even more emphatically by Johannes Reuchlin in 1504 in his *Art of Preaching (Liber congestorum de arte praedicandi)*. These admonitions are examples of the German humanists' concern not merely with learning for its own sake, but also with its bearing on faith and religion.

Albrecht von Eyb wrote his second major work in German and thereby addressed himself to an even broader group of readers, to persons who were at ease with their native language rather than with Latin. The *Book of Marriage* begins with an anecdote of a young man who asks the wise philosopher Socrates whether it is better to marry or to remain single. Socrates' answer is no answer at all; either alternative is undesirable. The *Book of Marriage*, very much like the *Pearl,* uses abundant citations, quotations and extracts from earlier writers, and Albrecht von Eyb's own library is again the source for much of the material used. Especially well represented are Valerius Maximus, Plautus, Terence, Petrarch and Pisani, but many other authors who were mentioned as sources of the *Pearl* reappear here. Added are a good number of amusing, sometimes bawdy stories, including the story of Guiscard and Ghismonde from the first novel of the fourth day of Boccaccio's *Decameron.* Albrecht von Eyb wrote the *Ehebuch* shortly before it appeared in print and it is possible that he realized that this work in the vernacular would reach a wide public through the medium of printing, as indeed it did. It was originally produced by Anton Koberger in Nuremberg in 1472 and reprinted thirteen times between that date and 1520. As in the case of the *Margarita* most of the fourteen editions of the *Book of Marriage* were produced by printers without any commitment to the promotion of humanist knowledge or ideas. Only two producers, Martin Landsberg in Leipzig and R. Paffraet in Deventer, can possibly be considered

progressives, while Johann Schönsperger in Augsburg, who produced six editions between 1482 and 1520, was a typical entrepreneur. Applying the same formula of an "average" of five hundred copies per edition to this work too, we reach the total of
seven thousand for the *Ehebuch*.

Granted that the topic itself and the entertaining stories made
the book popular, the readers nevertheless could not help learning
while enjoying. Knowledge of classical and humanist writers, here
presented in a palatable German rendering, acquainted groups of
readers with a literature which, without the help of books like
Eyb's *Ehebuch* (or Nicolaus von Wyle's or Heinrich Steinhöwel's
similar compilations), would never have reached them at the time.
The example of the *Ehebuch* belies the observations of so many
historians that only very few enlightened readers in Germany at
the end of the fifteenth and the beginning of the sixteenth centuries were at all familiar with the riches of classical literature.
The steadily increasing production of classical and humanist texts
in their original language *and* in translations, the surviving records
of importation of such writings into Germany, and the presence of
so many on the shelves of private, school, town and monastic
libraries even centuries after their publication is sufficient evidence
that the spread of humanism to countries beyond the Alps has all
too often been underestimated.

What conclusions about northern humanism can we reach from
the evidence of printed books? Though knowledge of classical
literature and learning had never really ceased during the Middle
Ages, it spread quickly with the rise of humanism in Italy. Contact
between south and north, always existing, increased during the
second half of the fourteenth and the first half of the fifteenth
centuries and thereafter, facilitating the transfer of some of the
ideas and the learning of Italian humanists to the north. Classical
and humanist manuscripts in Italy were copied by and for men
residing on the other side of the Alps, just as classical texts resting
in transalpine collections were copied and often removed in their
originals by Italians. But copying by hand was a tedious process,
and the total number of manuscripts which were available to the
apostles and disciples of humanism was limited.

Printing, perfected around the year 1450, greatly changed the
situation. Beginning in 1465 with the first publication of a classical
text (Cicero's *De officiis* in Mainz and Cologne), texts essential to

humanist studies were published in ever-increasing numbers in Italy and abroad, and were marketed on an almost international basis. Some of the northerners, imbued with the spirit of the Renaissance, used, extracted, and abstracted classical and humanist texts in their own compilations. These, together with vernacular translations of such texts, undoubtedly advanced the cause of humanism in German-speaking lands. The interest in improved grammar and style, and in the literature of the classics and of modern Italians, was promoted by the mass production of books, now usually issued in editions of several hundred copies. With the increase in the quantity of available books, bookselling grew and flourished. Without printing presses humanism in Germany would have progressed, but more haltingly. Without printing it seems improbable that Felix Fabri, traveler to Italy and the Holy Land, could have written toward the end of the fifteenth century with unbridled pride that "once upon a time Germany was poor in wisdom, power, and wealth; now it is not only equal to others in glorious work, but it surpasses loquacious Greece, proud Italy, and conquered aggressive France." Patriotic exaggeration, no doubt, but containing some truth! It would not be long before Aldo Manuzio, the great Venetian publisher of classics "at reasonable prices" and a staunch promoter of humanism, seriously considered moving to Germany (in 1505), and before the great humanists Reuchlin, Erasmus and Melanchthon would be judged by all as the equals of the best that Italy could offer.

BIBLIOGRAPHICAL NOTE: A useful introduction to the history of early printing is by Denys Hay, "Literature: the Printed Book," in the *New Cambridge Modern History, II: The Reformation* (Cambridge, 1962), 359–386. A general survey available to the student which includes the first century of printing is S. H. Steinberg, *Five Hundred Years of Printing* (Penguin Books. Baltimore, 1955). Also recommended is Curt F. Bühler, *The Fifteenth-Century Book* (Philadelphia, 1960). For a more detailed treatment of the general problems dealt with in this essay see R. Hirsch, *Printing, Selling and Readers* (Wiesbaden, 1967). The only comprehensive biography of Eyb is by Max Hermann, *Albrecht von Eyb und die Frühzeit des deutschen Humanismus* (Berlin, 1893).

THE ENGLISH
RENAISSANCE: SIR
THOMAS MORE
George Richard Potter

The English - speaking

people of the sixteenth century had their own Renaissance which went its own peculiar way and culminated in the genius of Shakespeare. It came almost unnoticed, heralded by a duke of Gloucester, an earl of Worcester, by bishops and abbots who wanted to be in the fashion—Whethamstede, Beckynton, Fleming, Free, Selling (or Tilley), Grey—and by the resident Italian Polydore Vergil. There was a printing press in Westminster in 1478, the year of More's birth; and before the fifteenth century was out, Erasmus was already in town. This base-born monk out of the cloister, Erasmus, was brought to England by his pupil-friend, the twenty-one year old Lord Mountjoy, who paid his expenses, and introduced him to the intellectual society at London and Oxford, and to More.

More was just twenty-one. He was the son of Judge More, an eminent and well-to-do lawyer, much respected in his profession, one of the select group of eminent civil servants whose portrait was delineated by the masterful hands of Hans Holbein. The boy, Tom, had been born and brought up in London and was sent to school there at the best academy for young gentlemen, St. Anthony's Threadneedle Street; and taken away at the age of twelve to enter the service, in the medieval sense, of John Morton, later

Cardinal of St. Anastasia, and who was then Archbishop of Canterbury and Lord Chancellor. The new page made an admirable
impression at Lambeth Palace, where he took part in some amateur
dramatics, overheard gossip about Richard III, and was highly
commended by his aged patron. The result was that a place was
found for him as soon as he was fourteen at Canterbury College,
Oxford, where he was one of a thousand or so young men at the
University, most of whom were preparing themselves for ordina-
tion. He had already learned enough Latin to understand the
elementary lectures which he attended. The Oxford interlude was
as short as that at Lambeth; he was soon back in London, where
he studied law for two years at the New Inn, one of the expensive
Inns of Chancery, as a kind of articled pupil, and was admitted to
Lincoln's Inn four days after his eighteenth birthday. He was to
follow his father's profession and this he did very successfully,
becoming an Utter (Outer) barrister in 1501, at the age of twenty-
three. His legal training was rapid and successful, and it must have
occupied most of his time and energies. It was all perfectly normal
and proper for the son of an eminent lawyer, and the young man
advanced rapidly in his chosen profession. These are basic facts
for the whole life that was to follow: a London boy who was very
seldom away from the metropolis, trained in the tough English
common law of the reign of Henry VII. It had not been an easy
life, but he had lived with gentlemen and had learned a good deal.
He was a good Latinist who could write a neat letter and he was
already in touch with Erasmus. To keep up with the intellectual
set he started to learn Greek from William Grocyn of New College,
Oxford, then lecturing in London. There were very few people in
England who knew this language, not more than ten, certainly,
altogether. It is this enthusiasm for letters and undoubted linguistic
ability which makes More quite exceptional. To learn Greek you
had to work it all out for yourself from the grammar of Manuel
Chrysoloras, Theodore Gaza, or Constantine Lascaris which had to
be brought from Venice or from the book fair at Frankfurt-am-
Main. Although later More was to be associated with some translations from Lucian's *Dialogues* he was not a serious Greek scholar;
the translations do not amount to very much. The important thing
is that he was identified with the new learning at an early age
and he was a Latinist.

The following years, to 1504, were of the utmost significance for
the future. His legal practice flourished from the beginning; his

voice was heard among the select advocates who appeared in West-minster Hall where everything was centralized—"for there was the seat of judgment and thither the tribes went up," as the historian Maitland remarked. Careless in his dress but scrupulous in his acceptance of clients, he was highly successful in a competitive business. Like many good lawyers he found time for other things, including love-making. His "youth had not been altogether blameless"; he was like other young men of his day and class.

The group he was in included Erasmus, John Colet, dean of St. Paul's, the Reverend Thomas Linacre, vicar of St. Lawrence Jewry, the Reverend Dr. Ruthall, and William Lily, rector of Holcot, Northamptonshire, and school master. They were much concerned about the state of the church and of education, as well as about the apocalyptic books supposed to have been written by Dionysius the Areopagite and, in the best medieval tradition, with the writings of St. Augustine. They were all learning Greek and talking about ancient Greek authors, Plato included. More himself gave some lectures on St. Augustine's *City of God* which attracted some attention. In 1501, he was well enough known to be invited to the wedding of Catherine of Aragon with the prince whom all hoped and expected would become King Arthur I.

Nor far from his office were the pleasant grounds of the Carthusian monks, the least corrupted of all the orders, and among them the young man found a welcome and congenial society, so much so that he nearly took the vows himself. He grew constant in prayer, contemplation, and in Bible study, and was practicing the conventional austerities, wearing a hair shirt, sleeping on bare boards without a pillow, observing days of fasting with great strictness, all commended by the church, although scarcely practiced by the pope of these years, Rodrigo Borgia, Alexander VI.

By Christmas of 1504 he had made up his mind that the contemplative life was not for him; he had been elected to Parliament and had found a young girl of barely past seventeen who would make a suitable wife—suitable in that she was almost illiterate, of gentle birth, and able to be molded to his pattern. There are some very curious passages about the marriage in Erasmus' colloquy, "The Uneasy Wife." Children came with the usual celerity—Margaret in 1505, Elizabeth in 1506, Cecily in 1507, and John in 1508. There was real affection, but it consorts well with the habits of the age when we learn that the first Mrs. More died when she was twenty-three and within a few days her husband remarried, this time a widow—*nec bella nec puella,* said the waspish Erasmus —who managed his household most efficiently.

Mr. More was indeed by now a busy man, politically, legalistically, intellectually. He had learned Greek well enough to be associated with the High Master of St. Paul's school in translating epigrams from the Greek anthology and with Erasmus in a small rendering of three *Dialogues* of Lucian, not a notably difficult author. Real linguistic ability there certainly was, as shown in verses and epigrams, letters and treatises in Latin, which he also spoke fluently. Later, as High Steward, an honorary office, of both Cambridge and Oxford universities, he had need of it and he showed a nice aptitude for legal Latin as well. Hebrew, apparently, he never attempted to master.

Most of all he liked, in his early days, lighthearted chatter in Latin with the handful of reputable scholars in constant correspondence one with another, frequently visiting his house, and of whom Erasmus was the most celebrated. More's renowned wit could be mordant as well as merry. When England and France were at war there was a close combat between two great ships of war, *Regent* and *Cordelière,* both of which were sunk, and both sides claimed a victory. A minor French humanist, de Brie (Brixius), wrote a poem of patriotic praise, More replied in kind, whereupon de Brie followed in *anti-Morus,* alleging that More's verses did not scan properly, to which the rejoinder was that de Brie was soft in the head and ill-mannered as well. There were to be others who were to feel the rough edge of More's tongue before long.

A good scholar and a very fine lawyer, he was Under Sheriff of London in 1510, having already had parliamentary experience, and in 1515 was sent on his first official mission abroad to represent, along with several prominent men, the English government in trade negotiations with the Netherlands, nominally with Prince Charles, the queen's young nephew and future Emperor Charles V. The conferences, after the manner of international gatherings, were expensive, prolonged and largely ineffective. More wrote to Erasmus:

I expected to be gone at most two months; but the embassy lasted more than six. . . . The office of ambassador has never held a great attraction for me. It does not suit us laymen as well as it does you clergy, for you either have no wives and children or you find them wherever you go. . . . A liberal allowance was granted to me by the king for the benefit of my retinue, but no consideration was made for those whom I had to leave at home; and although I am as you know, a kindly husband and an indulgent father and a gentle master, still I have never had the least success in persuading the members of my family to do without food, for my sake, until I came home. (*The Letters of Erasmus,* ed. F. M. Nichols [New York, 1904], II, 260.)

It was in this spirit of banter, and in the leisure of this enforced vacation abroad, that *Utopia* was born. It is More's chief title to fame and the chief stumbling block for the interpretation of his strange and complex character. For here we find a government servant and conservative lawyer, son of a judge of a supreme court, a rich and successful man of nearly forty, advocating, or seeming to advocate, communism. The humanist had studied his Plato, little known in the Middle Ages, and the earnest Christian had studied his New Testament, also little known in the Middle Ages; a happy society he concluded, like the early Christians, like a great monastery, should have all things in common. Many books have been written, and there are doubtless more to come, on the subject of *Utopia* and nothing like full justice can be done to it in an essay. What can be said is that it was published in Latin on the continent for a select group of specialists, that it was not unconnected with Erasmus' *In Praise of Folly (Encomium Moriae),* and that it was a satire, written before anyone had heard of Martin Luther.

It started a new *genre* of literature which has a continuous history; this was what heaven on earth could be: all dressing alike in a drab grey, having all meals together, with improving conversation led by the grave and reverend seniors. They work a six-hour day after which they "play two games not unlike chess. The first is a battle of numbers . . . the second is a game in which the vices fight a pitched battle with the virtues." (*Utopia,* II: 4, 144.)[1] If you don't like this you can work in your garden, for none must be idle.

The Utopians are very fond of gardens. In them they have vines, fruits, herbs, flowers, so well kept and flourishing that I never saw anything more fruitful and more tasteful anywhere. Their diligence in keeping them is increased not merely by the pleasure they afford them but by the keen competition between blocks as to which will have the best kept garden. (*Utopia,* II: 2, 131.)

In any satire it is likely to be difficult, if not impossible, to separate the serious from the intentionally transitory and entertaining—

[1] *Utopia,* Book II, ch. 4, p. 144. Source references will be given in this order, and henceforth in parentheses, in the text. The edition of the *Utopia* used here is that edited by J. H. Lupton (Oxford, 1895), which gives both the Latin and English texts.

who would try it for example with *Macbird?* To attempt it across the ages in dealing with a wit as lively and an intellect as keen and subtle as that of More, is to essay the impossible. In his own lifetime even his own family could not always tell when he was serious. *Utopia* was written in two sections, Book II coming before Book I, the abstract before the concrete.

It is well to realize that *Utopia* was conceived in practical terms. There was nothing wrong with war

to protect their own territory or to drive an invading enemy out of their friends' lands or, in pity for a people oppressed by tyranny, to deliver them by force of arms from the yoke and slavery of the tyrant. . . . They promise huge rewards to anyone who will kill the enemy king . . . they hire and send to war soldiers from all parts. . . . When cities are surrendered . . . they put to death the men who prevented surrender and make slaves of the rest. Whenever the natives [*indigeni*] have much unoccupied and uncultivated land, they found a colony. . . . If they resist, they wage war against them. They consider it a most just cause for war when a people which does not use its soil . . . forbids the use and possession of it to others. (*Utopia,* II: 5, 155; 8, 243ff.)

Part I is directly critical of sixteenth-century England where enclosures for sheep farming were depopulating my native Norfolk.

Your sheep that were wont to be so meek and tame, and so small eaters, now . . . be become so great devourers and so wild that they eat up and swallow down the very men themselves. They consume, destroy and devour whole fields, houses and cities. For look in what parts of the realm doth grow the finest and therefore dearest wool, there' noble men and gentlemen, yea and certain abbots, holy men God wot . . . leave no ground for tillage, they enclose all in pastures, they throw down houses, they pluck down towns and leave nothing standing but only the church, to make of it a sheep-house. (*Utopia,* I: 51, 52.)

This is not satire; it is crude economics and an implied plea for government intervention to inhibit private enterprise. It is part of a very eloquent passage showing a care for the weak and oppressed which was unusual in Renaissance England.

There was no balance of payments or currency problem in Utopia.

They do not use money themselves . . . gold and silver are so treated by them that no one values them more highly than their true nature deserves . . . from gold and silver they make chamber pots and all the humblest vessels for use everywhere . . . moreover they employ the same metals to make the chains and fetters which they put on their slaves. (*Utopia,* II: 6, 173 ff.)

Pearls, diamonds and rubies are given to little children which, when they grow up, they throw away like marbles, rattles, and dolls. If some of the learned commentators on *Utopia* could some-. times bring themselves to treat the book a little more light-heartedly, they might understand it, and More, and the English Renaissance, a little better.

There are, however, two matters included in it which have caused so much later discussion that to pass them over entirely, or to laugh them off, is impossible. In *Utopia* divorce for incompatibility of temper was allowed.

When a married couple agree insufficiently in their dispositions and both find others with whom they hope to live more agreeably, they separate by mutual consent and contract fresh unions, but not without the sanction of the senate. (*Utopia*, II: 7, 227.)

This, of course, was repugnant to canon law; but Henry VIII, who was at the height of his intellectual interests in 1516, must have read *Utopia* and therefore had reason later to look for a little help from the author in his own suit against Queen Catharine.

Secondly, there was religious toleration in the twentieth—at any rate the nineteenth—century use of the word. In *Utopia* it was

. . . especially ordained that it should be lawful for every man to follow the religion of his choice, that each might strive to bring others over to his own, provided that he quietly and modestly supported his own by reasons, nor bitterly demolished all others if his persuasions were not successful, nor used any violence, and refrained from abuse. (*Utopia*, II: 9, 271.)

There was, of course, no such toleration in any European country. "This realm," said Roper, More's son-in-law, himself once attracted to Lutheranism, "has so catholic a prince that no heretic durst show his face." "I pray God," was More's comment, "that some of us, as high as we seem to sit upon the mountains, treading heretics under our feet like ants, live not the day that we gladly would wish to be at a league and composition with them, to let them have their churches quietly to themselves, so that they would be content to let us have ours quietly to ourselves." (W. Roper, *Lyfe of Sir Thomas More*, ed. E. V. Hitchcock [London, 1935], p. 35.)

The two passages deserve to be considered side by side in the light of More's later career. Much of this can be summarized rapidly. On his return from the Netherlands he was again caught up in law and politics. He headed an advisory commission on civil disorders which reported on nationalist riots in the city streets in 1517, when the mob looked like it was getting out of hand but did not. It was just as well, for as the disputed Shakespearean play *Sir Thomas More* put it, "For other ruffians, as their fancies wrought with self-same hand, self-reasons and self-right, would shark on you, and men like ravenous fishes would feed on one another."

He represented the pope's envoy in a maritime dispute, he was Master of Requests, in charge of an important prerogative court in this same year 1517, went on an embassy to Calais, and most significant of all, became a member of the Council, the Privy Council as it was soon to be known. The king, perhaps at Wolsey's[2] suggestion, knew where to turn for advice and after that there was no looking back. In 1520 More was present at the conspicuous prestige expenditure of the Field of Cloth of Gold, had some more commercial business, and by 1521 was treasurer of the Exchequer. He was by now a rich man and able to buy property in the city and later a large house in the country for his growing family. The twenties were years of rapid and deserved success. Everything he did prospered. He delivered public addresses to the young Emperor Charles V, who was much impressed; he carried on a great deal of letter-writing and office business; he flattered the much-flattered Wolsey, to whom he was "your humble orator and most bounden beadsman" until he fell from power, when it became a very different story; he was elected speaker of the House of Commons in April 1523, where he did something to secure freedom of speech and all that that later implied. Money had to be found for a war in France. Henry VIII was a hawk and More was a spokesman for the doves, but "the war," we read, "seemed like ending in stalemate," and increased war taxation was as inevitable as it was unpopular. More had to assist in this.

The king now liked More's company; a favorite pastime was to walk in the garden with his heavy arm around More's neck. But More knew what this was worth. He commented to Roper: "I find his grace my very good lord indeed, and I believe he doth as singularly favor me as any subject within this realm. Howbeit . . . I have no cause to be proud thereof, for if my head could win him a castle in France . . . it should not fail to go. . . ." (Roper, *Sir*

[2] Thomas Wolsey (1475?–1530), bishop of Lincoln, archbishop of York, cardinal, chief minister to Henry VIII, for whom he failed to secure a divorce from Catharine of Aragon; died while under arrest for treason.

Thomas More, p. 21.) High steward of the University of Oxford
(1524), where some recalcitrant dons needed to be coerced into
the Erasmian conception of good letters, high steward of Cambridge (1525), which was then safe in the humanist hands of
Fisher,[3] More became chancellor of the Duchy of Lancaster in the
same year with responsibilities for administering an enormous
block of royal territory. He became, finally, the keeper of the king's
conscience, Lord Chancellor, in October 1529.

The great silver seal of England, without which the machinery
of state could not function, was in his hands, and almost his first
duty was to summon and to preside over the Parliament—the
Reformation Parliament—which later decided to dissolve the
monasteries, in spite of the fact that the bishops and abbots together had a majority in the House of Lords. It was a notable innovation for a layman to be given the office of Lord Chancellor, but
the king was well aware that his new chancellor had plenty of
theological interests and was very competent to speak about matters which were likely to receive much attention. Luther was one
subject of attention; the suit for nullity brought against Catharine,
which not even Wolsey had been able to settle, was another.

As early as 1521, the year in which Mr. More became Sir Thomas
More, Henry VIII had refuted Luther's pamphlet on the Baby-
lonish Captivity in his booklet, *Assertio Septem Sacramentotum,*
of which More was, in his own words, "a sorter out and placer of
the principal matters therein contained." (Roper, *Sir Thomas More,*
p. 67.) Luther rudely answered back, and More, equally rudely,
wrote a rejoinder in Latin in 212 closely printed columns. It has
never been translated, nor need it be, for much of what it said,
in the immortal phrase of Gibbon, is better left "veiled in the
obscurity of a learned language." It marked, nonetheless, the start
of religious controversy to which More was thus urged on by the
bishop of London: "Since you, dearest brother, are distinguished
as a second Demosthenes in our native language as well as in Latin,
you cannot better occupy your spare time . . . than in publishing
something in English which will reveal to simple and uneducated
men the crafty wickedness of the heretics, and will better equip
such folk against such impious supplanters of the church."

The result of this was a torrent of prose, some of it still only to

[3] John Fisher (1459–1535), bishop of Rochester, chancellor of Cambridge University, president of Queens' College, Cambridge, active supporter of the new
learning, wrote against Luther, opposed divorce of Henry VIII.

be read in the rare edition of More's works published by William Rastell in 1557—"a million words," says a modern biographer, R. W. Chambers. They helped to establish standard English. They showed the wonderful possibilities of the vernacular at a time when most educated people thought the vernacular fit only for the lower orders, and they also reveal a little—for nothing can reveal the whole—of More's innermost thoughts about the spiritual life which was his constant care. The *Dialogue Concerning Heresies* (1528), the *Supplication of Souls* (1529), the *Confutation of Tyndate's Answer* (1532–33), the *Reply to Frith's Treatise on the Sacrament* (1532–33), the *Apology* (1533), the *Debellation of Salem and Bizance* (1533), the *Dialogue of Comfort* (1534), and the *Treatise on the Passion* (1534) were interspersed by some purely devotional literature. Some of it is tedious, some of it is special pleading, some hardly logical, some merely abusive. But it is all shot through with passionate religious fervor intensified by reflection. Heresy, and therefore heretics, he detested; he was in his own words "to . . . heretics grievous." Around this phrase and its implications a controversy developed: the contrast between the toleration of *Utopia* and the torture and burning of heretics was too great to escape later comment. More saw nothing wrong in the agonies of death by burning for refusing to accept transubstantiation; the other side of the story is to be read in the *Acts and Monuments* of John Foxe, in the *Book of Martyrs,* which is now more esteemed than it was forty years ago.

More had leisure to write in these last years because he had joined the opposition. If the king was to marry Anne Boleyn to bring national security by begetting a male heir, the authority of the pope must be repudiated. And so it came to pass; on January 26, 1533, Sir Thomas Audley became Lord Chancellor; on April 17, 1534, More was taken into custody for refusing to take the oath required by the Act of Succession of 1534. In the sixteenth century, the alternative to support of the government was opposition, and opposition, as was well known, meant death. You could not resign and attack the government from the opposition benches. Opposition meant rebellion such as that which flared up in Lincolnshire a month after More died, or it meant the conquest of England by a foreign army such as Fisher was asking for. You must either go with the government or else, like Reginald Pole,[4] live abroad.

---

[4] Reginald Pole (1500–1558), cardinal, archbishop of Canterbury, opponent of Henry VIII; reconciled England to Rome in 1556.

It was not, however, easy to prove that the greatest lawyer in England had committed technical high treason, and a clumsy attempt to use his association with the Nun of Kent and to remove him by Act of Attainder (the weapon to be used by Parliament later against its rivals) failed. There had to be a public trial in Westminster Hall before a jury, and even then the prosecution had in the end to rely upon the dubious testimony (or perjury) of Sir Richard Rich, who was himself to become Lord Chancellor from 1547 to 1552 under Edward VI. Still, the formalities of the law were followed, he was convicted, and the king mercifully allowed the swift death by the axe.

In 1551, sixteen years after More's death, Ralph Robinson prefixed to the first English translation of *Utopia* a letter to Mr. William Cecil, later the great Lord Burghley:

For the excellent qualities, wherewith the great goodness of God had plentifully endowed him, and for the high place and room, whereunto his prince had most graciously called him, [he was] notably well known, not only among us his countrymen, but also in foreign countries and nations; therefore I have not much to speak of him.

This only I say: that it is much to be lamented of all, and not only of us English men, that a man of so incomparable wit, of so profound knowledge, of so absolute learning, and of so fine eloquence was yet nevertheless so much blinded, rather with obstinacy than with ignorance, that he could not, or rather would not, see the shining light of God's holy truth in certain principal points of Christian religion; but did rather choose to persevere and continue in his wilful and stubborn obstinacy even to the very death: this I say is a thing much to be lamented. (*Utopia*, p. 17.)

There are still more than several unsolved questions about the life of More. That he was a saint, in the common meaning of that word, and in the technical meaning of the word, no one would deny. The lives of the saints, most of whom worked miracles, constitute the peculiar historical *genre* known as hagiography. What of twentieth-century hagiography? There are a score of lives of More, written in many cases for the edification of the faithful. The twentieth-century lives of More vary relatively little in their factual content, but they vary tremendously in their emphasis and commentary. More was a great man, but he was also part of a great age, that of the Renaissance and the Reformation. To see him in isolation is wrong, for he chose to live in society, to mingle actively in law and politics. It is what he meant for his own age that it is for the historian to attempt to expound; hagiography is not enough.

BIBLIOGRAPHICAL NOTE: The literature relating to More is considerable; Conyers Read, *Bibliography of British History: Tudor Period,* 1485–1603, mentions all the important books published before 1956 (2nd ed., Oxford, 1952). There are numerous biographies of varying merit of which T. E. Bridgett, *The Life of Blessed Thomas More* (1891) and R. W. Chambers, *Thomas More* (1935), are good and sympathetic. *The Life of Sir Thomas More* by William Roper edited by E. V. Hitchcock (1935) is the chief semi-contemporary source; the *Letters of Sir Thomas More* are edited by E. F. Rogers (New Haven, 1937), supplemented by H. Schalte Herbruggen, *Sir Thomas More, Neue Briefe* (Münster, 1966). More's complete writings are in course of publication by the Yale University Press. The standard edition of *Utopia,* Latin and English was that edited by J. H. Lupton, Oxford, 1895.

MACHIAVELLI
Felix Gilbert

Since Machiavelli's death

in 1527, an unending stream of books, treatises and articles on his ideas and writings has poured forth. Inevitably, one cannot speak about Machiavelli's ideas without discussing why his work has aroused such passionate excitement. The following essay deals, first, with Machiavelli's ideas, and secondly, with the reasons for the excitement which they have caused. There seems good reason to undertake such a discussion at this time because of what seems to me a particular affinity of our time with the issues and problems by which Machivelli was confronted and which he attacked.

In the history of political thought Machiavelli was a revolutionary. The ideas which he pronounced were challenges to the notions of the century in which he wrote, and still more to those of the centuries which preceded his. The audacity of Machiavelli's challenge can be fully gauged only if we have an idea of what his contemporaries thought about politics and social order. And this is where the experiences of our own time can be of use. After two world wars, in which the struggle of expanding sovereign nation-states, living in "international anarchy," has wrought endless misery on the world, we are anxious for the creation of an international society, encompassing the entire globe, and settling conflicts by peaceful means. After experiencing the horrors to which totalitarianism can lead, we are profoundly conscious of the need for the supremacy of law in political and social life. There were also the ideas and ideals which constituted the basic, assumptions of political thought before Machiavelli wrote. Then the world was viewed as one great unified society, as a *corpus Christianum* or as a *res publica Christiana*. Within this hierarchically organized, all-embracing society, with emperor and pope at its head, individual rulers and governments had one supreme task, the maintenance of justice. "The maintenance of justice includes everything," to use a phrase that was frequently employed at this time. Government was identified with the administration of justice.

Certainly, political reality in the centuries preceding the Renaissance did not consist purely of peace and law. Books have been written about "Machiavellism before Machiavelli," showing the cool and ruthless pursuit of political aims in the Middle Ages and in the Renaissance. It has been said with some justification that Machiavelli merely described what went on in his own time and codified its practice in his writings. Yet, although political practice differed from the ideal of a society in which various political states were peacefully united, and in which the individual lived securely under the shield of justice, the manner in which men acted in practical politics was never defended as right or just. On the contrary, it was viewed as a deviation from what ought to be: it was a sign of man's sinfulness. In the course of time awareness of the distance which separated political practice from political ideals increased. Yet far into the sixteenth century and beyond Machiavelli's time, there was no doubt that the moral duty of princes and governments was to administer justice and to pursue the ideal of a perfect Christian society. Luther believed in the reality and necessity of an all-embracing *corpus Christianum;* the events of the sixteenth and seventeenth centuries, the vehemence of the religious wars, are incomprehensible if we do not take into account that a break-up of the all-comprehensive *res publica Christiana* was regarded as unthinkable. Machiavelli's contemporary, Thomas More, one of the keenest observers of the contemporary scene, had so few illusions about the ways of the world and of the men of the world that he placed his perfect society outside the known globe; but the notions on which his outline of life in Utopia were based were the traditional ideals of a social order in which men would live in peace and justice. Gasparo Contarini, the Venetian statesman and reforming cardinal, praised Venice because it had an

excellent system of justice and because its citizens detested soldier-
ing; Venice, according to Contarini, should be an example to the
other states of the world. Erasmus hoped that if such ideas were
inculcated in Christian princes through education, they would set
the world on a right and true course. And to turn from the writers
on politics to the actors in politics: Was the establishment of an
integrated, peaceful Christian world not the task with which Emperor Charles V exhausted himself so that finally he gave up the
struggle and retired to the monastery of San Juste?

He realized this was'nt working

If we realize that in Machiavelli's time thinking about politics
and the problems of the social order was dominated by the notion
of a hierarchically organized Christian world in which the task
of princes and governments was the distribution of justice, then we
can appreciate the audacity of the ideas which Machiavelli advanced: According to him the permanent character of political life
was not peace but struggle. The crucial factor in politics was not
justice but power.

This was the core of Machiavelli's doctrine. He stated these
basic ideas at once in the first chapter of the *Discorsi*[1] when he
discussed the beginnings of cities. He wrote: "Men cannot make
themselves safe except with power." Therefore, cities should be
placed "in very fertile places where, since the richness of the site
permits the city to expand, she can both defend herself from those
who assail her and crush whoever opposes himself to her greatness." Machiavelli's insistence on the unavoidability of strife and
tension in the relations among states contains two elements. The
one is the assumption that (*Discorsi*, Ch. 6) "all human affairs
are in motion, ever in a state of flux, and cannot stand still; thus,
either there will be improvement or decline." No social body can
remain unchanged and stable. Either a state will grow and expand,
or it will be destroyed by others. States must be organized in such
a way that they are able to conquer and to expand. States are like
plants; they grow, filling out more space, or they die of suffocation
if they cannot rise to light. To Machiavelli the struggle of a state
against others for territorial conquests is a law of nature.

Machiavelli's idea of the inevitable trend toward expansion and
aggression was founded also on his notion of the character of man.

[1] The translation of Machiavelli's works used here is by Allan Gilbert (Durham,
1965).

It contained a psychological element. Aggression and expansion result from the inborn drives of human nature: "Truly it is very natural and normal to wish to conquer and when men do it who can, they always will be praised or not blamed." (*Prince*, Ch. 3).

Because Machiavelli regarded an aggressive drive to be inherent in human psychology, he viewed not only the relations among states but also the relations among individuals within states as determined by a struggle for superiority. Nobody should rely on the loyalty or selflessness of men. They are all egoists "eager for gain." That is the basis of his famous thesis that "it is much safer to be feared than loved": "Men have less hesitation in injuring one who makes himself loved than one who makes himself feared. For love is held by a chain of duty which, since men are bad, they break at every chance for their own profit. But fear is held by a dread of punishment that never fails you." (*Prince*, Ch. 17).

The life of states as well as the life of individuals within states is a competitive struggle fought out with all possible means, and is won by those who have the greatest power. Not justice but power is of paramount importance in the ordering of social life.

In modern language power is a term of a complex character: manifestations of power are found in the most divergent phenomena—in the workings of nature as well as in the workings of the mind—in electricity and in persuasion. If Machiavelli spoke of political life as being a struggle for power he used power in an almost primitive sense: the ability of imposing one's will upon others by means of force. For this reason he regarded control of strong military forces as the most important ingredient of political power. Machiavelli had a consuming interest in military affairs. He had very pronounced views about weapons and fortifications, about strategy and tactics and liked to present himself in his writings as a military expert. Nevertheless, as much as Machiavelli was attracted by the details of military organization and warfare, this was not the primary reason for his interest in military affairs. He regarded soldiers as instruments for obtaining, holding, and expanding power—briefly, as the decisive factors in politics.

Machiavelli was a great admirer of ancient Rome, and his *Discorsi* are a codification of the rules of political behavior which can be deduced from Roman history. Such admiration for the classical world, of course, was a common intellectual attitude in the Renaissance. Yet in Machiavelli's writings the admiration of Rome had a concrete and practical aspect. He admired the Roman polit-

ical successes and the expansion of Roman power over the world
resulting from the excellence of the Roman military organization,
and his interest in this organization was the center of Machiavelli's
admiration for Rome. Nevertheless, it would not be fair to ascribe
to Machiavelli too primitive a notion of power. He was aware that
the maintenance of power involved complicated issues. How could
a commander be secure in his hold over his troops? How could a
ruler be safe in the possession of power? Machiavelli deduced
from the Roman example that stabilization of power required a
molding of the minds of those who were to obey. The Romans
taught the importance of education and training, of discipline, of
the coordination of military and political organization. These were
the positive means by which a collective spirit of submissiveness
could be created. But a spirit of obedience could also be produced
negatively be instilling fear of punishment for disobedience or
revolt in the soldiers or in the populace.

Machiavelli presented his views on this issue in the seventeenth
chapter of the *Prince,* where he discussed how it was possible that
Hannibal "though he had a very large army—a mixture of countless sorts of men—led to service in foreign lands" maintained order
so that "no discord ever appeared in his army." Machiavelli's answer to this question was: "This could not have resulted from anything else than Hannibal's well-known inhuman cruelty which,
together with his numberless abilities, made him always respected
and terrible in the soldiers' eyes. Without it his other abilities
would not have been enough to get that result." This will have
shown what is meant by the statement that Machiavelli placed
power in the center of politics. His concept of power was simpler
and more concrete than ours. It implied a relationship in which
one party was stronger than the other and in which the stronger
was in possession of the means to establish and maintain his superiority. The primary instrument to keep power was force, but
because Machiavelli realized that the maintenance of power could
also be effected by other means, by institutions, disciplinary rules,
law, psychological pressure, he pointed the way to a somewhat
more complex notion of this concept.

Evidently, in order to arrive at results and conclusions almost
diametrically opposed to those held in his time and before, Machiavelli had to use a different way of arguing—new methods. Whether
Machiavelli was right in his views about the nature of politics
might be subject to debate. Unquestionably he has exerted a pro-

found and lasting influence on our thinking about politics through
the methods which he employed.

Machiavelli's most important methodical innovation is indicated
in the famous sentence from the dedication of the *Prince* in which
he stated that his most treasured possession, which he had incorporated in his treatise, was his "understanding of great men's
actions, gained in lengthy experience with recent events and in
continual reading of ancient ones." According to Machiavelli, the
doctrines of theology and the teachings of moral philosophy lacked
validity in the field of politics. The area from which a thinker
could deduce prescriptions and rules for the conduct of politics
was the experience of the past. History offered the material with
which Machiavelli built his new political laws. Up to very recently
the methods of political science have remained to a large extent
historical.

Machiavelli gave a new methodical basis to political science not
only by the way in which he used history; his writings suggested
another departure: Political thinking ought to be concerned not
exclusively with forms of government, with institutions and organizations, but also with the individuals who composed the body
politic. Political action had the effect of changing a factual situation,
and it also had a psychological aspect. It patterned the mind of the
ruled. The best-known chapters of the *Prince*—best-known because the most shocking—are the chapters fifteen through nine-
teen, in which Machiavelli discussed the qualities which a prince
ought to have. They do not offer what their theme promises: the
outline of the image of an ideal ruler. They study the effects which
the behavior of a prince might have on the attitude of the ruled
toward the ruler. They emphasize the importance of psychological
factors in politics. Of course, these are very small beginnings when
we consider the roles which social psychology and the psychology
of personality play in modern political science. But here again it
might be said that Machiavelli pointed the way.

The realization of the paramount importance of power in politics,
the shifting of political argumentation from theology and moral
philosophy to history and psychology, were discoveries of a revolutionary character. But do these achievements fully explain the
excitement which Machiavelli's writings have caused, the flood of
books and discussions which surround his name? Why has he
aroused more interest and more passion than those political
thinkers whose achievement can be compared to his—St. Augustine, Rousseau, or even Marx?

This question might be clarified if we consider Machiavelli's
writings not in technical terms—not in their bearing on the development of political science—but if, instead, we examine the general view of the world which stands behind these theories. If
Machiavelli was right, if his views on politics were true, what was
the political and social world in which man lived? It was a world
in which nothing was constant and everything was fluid, in which
states were rising and falling because, like plants, they were growing up, reaching their apex, and then slowly declining. If man
was born into the time of the decline of a state he could have little
hope for a life of fame, of satisfaction or security. Moreover, man
found himself in permanent anxiety. Everyone was struggling to
get to the top and that meant that each looked upon all others as
rivals in a hostile way. In these struggles, whether among individuals or among states, every weapon was permitted and no pardon
was given. The victory belonged to those who were strongest, and
even of this there was no guarantee because the accidents to
which physical nature was exposed occurred also in human affairs; *Fortuna* ruled over the fate of men and of states. This was
a world without justice; nor was there hope for compensation in
a world beyond. It was a pitiless world without love or charity,
without restraints of religion or traditional moral philosophy. Was
it possible to conceive living in such a world? In the Middle Ages
this question would have been answered with a categorical no.
Since the Renaissance, however, life became increasingly secu-
larized, it was seen less as ruled by a divine providence directing
it toward a final aim. The question how people could live in a
world no longer subordinated to a religious order of values had
become meaningful and urgent. Because Machiavelli was the first
political thinker who envisaged the world without hope for stability, without the cement of morality, his thought has been a starting
point for the examination of the fundamental problems of a secular
world. In discussing Machiavelli's ideas, people discussed a problem of general human concern.

Although interest in Machiavelli has continued unabated in the
more than four hundred years that have passed since his death,
his political ideas have been subjected to widely differing interpretations. It has rightly been said that changes in the climate of the
time brought about these differences in interpretation. The religious spirit of the age of the Counter-Reformation saw this advocate
of a disregard for religious prescripts as an embodiment of evil.

The age of absolutism (seventeenth and eighteenth centuries) was puzzled and fascinated by Machiavelli's views on princeship. The nationalistic spirit of the nineteenth century saw in Machiavelli primarily a prophet of the national state. In totalitarian times Machiavelli's writing attracted attention as a handbook of political techniques.

But there is a common thread which runs through these changing interpretations. All of them attempted to show that Machiavelli did not really mean what he seemed to say. All these interpretations assumed that it was not possible for a human being to live without any belief, only with the view that the world was nothing but a deadly struggle in which the strongest had the best chances, in which the outcome remained uncertain and victory ephemeral. Machiavelli must have had some higher aims; he must have had some positive beliefs—that was the assumption—and these various interpretations looked for the values which Machiavelli recognized as binding and which he wanted to achieve through recommendations of an extreme character. From this point of view it was appropriate that, in the later sixteenth century, when religion was man's main concern, this protagonist of a purely secular point of view was simply not recognized as being human; he became "Old Nick" the devil, or a magician, as in Marlowe's *Jew of Malta.* In the eighteenth century people denied that Machiavelli could have been in earnest when he set forth the amoral doctrines of the *Prince.* It was suggested that, on the contrary, he had highly moral and praiseworthy intentions: By giving the Medici rulers the advice which he offered in the *Prince,* Machiavelli made sure that the Medici would introduce an unbearable tyranny, would become despised and would be overthrown; the secret of the *Prince,* its real purpose, was to lead to the foundation of a free republic in Florence; these were the aims of Machiavelli in writing this poisonous book. These eighteenth-century interpreters of Machiavelli's thought were upset and disappointed when letters to his friend Vettori appeared, showing that Machiavelli was earnestly seeking to regain the favor of the Medici and that he meant most seriously the recommendations made in the *Prince.* Their disappointment was soon overshadowed, however, by the discovery of the nationalistic note in the last chapter of the *Prince.* To the nineteenth century this chapter provided a full explanation of the amoral character of Machiavelli's strange treatise; Machiavelli's aim was patriotic: He wanted Italy's national unification. But— to use the famous formula of the German historian Ranke—"the

Italian situation was so desperate that Machiavelli was daring enough to prescribe poison." Only the energy of a despotic ruler could unify this disintegrating society. Under twentieth-century totalitarianism, the nationalistic tone of this interpretation was somewhat played down; instead emphasis was placed on the notion that Machiavelli had established the autonomy of politics. Politics had its own ethics and could command freely and fully over the individual. Christian religion was replaced by a political religion; the state was the embodiment of all ethical demands.

In the light of modern critical scholarship, the various interpretations of Machiavelli's thought which have been given in the course of the last five centuries seem one-sided and simplified. Nevertheless, the long search for the values behind Machiavelli's theories has demonstrated that he had positive aims and recognized higher values. He esteemed freedom, he praised willingness to sacrifice one's life for one's fatherland, he appreciated the courage of men who stood up against fate: Briefly, if he denied the old gods, he did not imply that there were no gods at all.

Therefore, although modern historical scholarship rejects most of the interpretations of Machiavelli's thought given in the past and applies different methods, it recognizes the importance of the question with which previous centuries were concerned: What did Machiavelli, who condemned all traditional aims and values, acknowledge to be the goals to which man ought to aspire? This characterization of the aims of today's Machiavelli scholarship may sound strange because, at first glance, it may appear to be concerned with rather minute questions which it investigates with microscopic accuracy: Were the *Prince* and the *Discorsi* composed simultaneously or with an interval of two or three years? Was the *Prince* composed in stages or did Machiavelli have a detailed outline of the entire work in mind from the outset? What is the meaning of the word *stato* in Machiavelli's writings? Which classical writers did he know? Although these questions appear to be almost picayune, they have their bearing on the problem of Machiavelli's fundamental aims and values. For instance, if the composition of the *Discorsi* followed that of the *Prince* by two or three years, then the *Prince*, written soon after Machiavelli's release from prison, might have been composed under duress in order to gain the favor of the Medici, whereas the *Discorsi*, with their advocacy of republican freedom, might present Machiavelli's true ideals. If the two works originated at the same time as different facets of the same conception, however, Machiavelli's favoring a free republic in the *Discorsi* becomes less significant. The question of the structure of the *Prince* is important because it tries to determine whether the last chapter, with its appeal for the liberation of Italy from the barbarians, forms an integral part of the work or is a later, somewhat rhetorical addition. In the latter case it would not be justified to give much weight to the role of nationalism in Machiavelli's thought. The use of the word *stato* in Machiavelli's writings has aroused so much interest because the meaning of this term changed just at this time. It had indicated "those who are in power," but it began now to receive the modern meaning, "everyone and everything living under the same government." If for Machiavelli *stato* meant what we understand by state, he might have ascribed to politics not only autonomy but a morality of its own. This again is connected with the question whether his acquaintance with classical writings was intimate enough to have him reject the Christian religion in favor of pagan ethics.

Modern scholarship has not solved these questions, at least not in the sense that scholars have achieved general agreement on any of them. But these studies and investigations have increased our knowledge of the intellectual milieu in which Machiavelli's ideas arose and have indicated the difficulties of the problem for which previous centuries had definite answers because they applied to it their own scale of values. Machiavelli as prophet of nationalism, Machiavelli as advocate of a non-Christian political ethic, Machiavelli as man of firm republican principles—all these formulations do not do justice to the complexity of his political thought. Because his ideas cannot be smoothly fitted into any of these categories, it would appear that the questions which they raise were not Machiavelli's central concern, and it might be suggested that, in order to comprehend his basic aim, one has to go beyond the problem of the moral values in political life and to focus on what he regarded as the fundamental element of all political relationships. The overriding issue in all of Machiavelli's writings is the relation of the ruler to the ruled. Between the ruler—who might be one man or an entire class—and the ruled there is a natural antagonism. In his two chief works, the *Prince* and the *Discorsi,* Machiavelli wants to demonstrate how this antagonism can be overcome so that, instead of being weakened by this conflict, the power of the social body—of the state—will be increased. In the *Prince* Machiavelli explains that, for the purpose of solidifying the state under a one-man rule, a prince might have to take recourse to deceit, lies, and cruelty. In the *Discorsi* he shows that the natural enmity between the ruling group and the ruled must be turned into vitalizing competition by means of severe but equal and impartial laws. In both cases the result will be an increase in power of the social body.

But it might appear that we are now thrown back to the same problem with which previous centuries have been vainly struggling: What is the purpose of this increase in power? What are the aims or what are the values for which power should be used? Here it might be helpful to consider once again Machiavelli's model for a perfect political organization: the Roman Republic. The most noticeable sign of the excellence of the Roman system was that Rome had gained a large number of military triumphs and conquered the entire globe. But Rome possessed still another distinguishing feature: the length of its existence. It is true that at the end Rome too had declined and fallen, as all things must do. But it had staved off its decline longer than any other state. For some time at least Rome seemed to have triumphed over nature and controlled events. Machiavelli has no illusions: The natural cycle of birth, growth, decline, and death cannot be broken. But he believed that, for a time at least, correctly organized and concentrated power can slow down the process. In the sense that power might enable man to control events it gives him the possibility of triumphing over nature and of demonstrating his freedom. To return from this modern terminology to the images in which Machiavelli expressed these ideas: Whoever can control events, whether individual or people, has virtue (*virtù*). And, as Machiavelli emphasized in the famous twenty-fifth chapter of the *Prince, Fortune's Power in Human Affairs and How She Can be Forestalled:* "Fortune may be mistress of one-half of our actions. But she leaves the other half almost under our control."

The fleeting moments of control may seem a meager compensation for the violence, the cruelty, the brutality involved in the recognition of the rule of power in politics. But this might not have seemed so to Machiavelli, and we might be able to understand this better than previous centuries. If we consider the malaise of our time as it has developed over the last twenty or thirty years, we are distressed by our impotence to influence a government machine which seems to be moving of its own weight. We are desperate about the manner in which we are inextricably drawn into conflicts by a chain of events, the beginnings of which are quite outside our lives. We are frightened by the new horizons which, against our will, science is opening to us. We feel powerless and ever anxious to regain some control over our existence.

The feeling of having lost control over events was dominant in the last years of the Italian Renaissance, in those decades when Machiavelli lived. He was twenty-five when, in 1494, the French appeared in Italy. From then on the circumscribed sphere in which Italian politics had previously been acted out and had enjoyed autonomy was broken. The Italian states became pawns in a game played by greater powers which the Italians were unable to control or to influence. The half century following the French invasion was a repeated demonstration of Italian helplessness. Machiavelli had no doubts that, on this new political scene which had opened with the French invasion, the old political precepts and notions were of no avail any longer. They had to be swept away as valueless. One had to begin anew to learn about politics: One had to study—to quote from the fifteenth chapter of the *Prince,* in which Machiavelli explains the novelty of his approach—"how men live" and not "how they ought to live." But because man was a rational being, this disillusioned consideration of things as they are might teach man for a fleeting but glorious moment the possibility of controlling events and of asserting his freedom. From this desperation and from this hope there arose the revolution in political thought which is connected with the name of Machiavelli.

BIBLIOGRAPHICAL NOTE: The standard biography of Machiavelli is the one by Roberto Ridolfi which was translated into English and published by the Chicago University Press in 1963. Ridolfi's book is chiefly concerned with Machiavelli's political and literary career but does not provide an extensive analysis of Machiavelli's thought. For these problems see John R. Hale, *Machiavelli and Renaissance Italy* (New York, 1960), and Felix Gilbert, *Machiavelli and Guicciardini* (Princeton, 1965). The chief works of Machiavelli have been translated by Allan Gilbert and were published in three volumes by the Duke University Press in 1965. An English translation of the *Discorsi* with extensive comments was edited by Leslie J. Walker and published by the Yale University Press in 1950. The *Prince* and the *Discorsi* are available in a Modern Library edition.

PIUS II AND THE RENAISSANCE PAPACY
※ Robert Schwoebel

Complaining to a group

of cardinals about the widespread criticism of the papacy and the
lack of respect and obedience shown it by princes and people,
Pope Pius II (1458–64) declared: "If we send envoys to ask aid of
sovereigns, they are laughed at. If we impose tithes on the clergy,
they appeal to a future council. If we issue indulgences and encourage the contribution of money by spiritual gifts, we are accused
of avarice. People think our sole object is to amass gold. No one
believes what we say. Like insolvent tradesmen we are without
credit. Everything we do is interpreted in the worst way." (*Commentaries,* VII, 516.)[1]

Time has not worked to improve the reputation of the papacy
of the fifteenth and early sixteenth centuries. In textbooks and
general treatments of the period the popes are still presented as
the villains of the Renaissance. Who has not heard of the three evil
geniuses, as they have been called, who ruled successively as bishops of Rome from 1492 until 1521? Alexander VI (1492–1503)—
Rodrigo Borgia before becoming pope—is universally regarded as
the most immoral man ever to have occupied the See of St. Peter.

[1] *The Commentaries of Pius II,* Book VII, p. 516. Source references will be given
in this order and in parentheses in the text. The edition used here is that edited and
translated by F. A. Gragg and L. C. Gabel, Smith College Studies in History, North-
ampton, 1936–1957.

His amorous adventures, the orgies over which he presided in the Vatican, and the political uses to which he put his illegitimate offspring have made the name Borgia a synonym for the word iniquity. Julius II (1503–13), immortalized by a scathing dialogue, the *Julius Excluded from Heaven* (usually attributed to the famous humanist Erasmus), is remembered not only for his vigorous pros-ecution of Rome's political interests, but for the fact that he donned the armor of a warrior, and, though the spiritual head of Christendom, personally commanded his armies in battles against other Christian powers. Leo X (1513–21), the third of our infamous triumvirate, though credited with being a man of peace and refined tastes, is accused of being so preoccupied with the art, literature, music, and drama of the Renaissance that he paid little heed to reports of Luther's defiance in Germany and thus let slip the oppor-tunity to preserve the unity of the church.

Though less notorious the fifteenth-century predecessors of these three have been viewed generally in the same light. Nicholas V (1447–55), the founder of the Vatican Library and an eminent humanist, has been criticized for his scholarly leanings and his concern for rebuilding Rome in the style of the Renaissance at that moment when Constantinople, the capital of the Christian East, fell into the hands of the Ottoman Turks. Calixtus III (1455–58), who prosecuted the war against the Moslems, is disliked because he practiced a stern religion, and because he, a Borgia, established his relatives in Italy. Paul II (1464–71) is dismissed summarily as "a luxury-loving Venetian," and Innocent VIII (1484–92), as "weak, compliant, and undistinguished." On the other hand the sins and crimes of Sixtus IV (1471–84) are usually chronicled in detail. A vigorous advocate of the political rights of the papacy in Italy, he was an opponent of Lorenzo de'Medici and is especially condemned for his alleged involvement in a conspiracy with the Pazzi, a bank-ing family of Florence, to overthrow the Medici dynasty. The scheme collapsed when the Pazzi failed to murder Lorenzo while the latter was taking communion in the cathedral of Florence. Lorenzo's brother, Giuliano, however, was killed by two priests, and the wrath of the city fell upon the Pazzi and their adherents. The pope's association with the Pazzi in matters of banking and politics was enough to make him guilty by association. Curiously the whole story is yet to be told.

The trouble with much of this kind of criticism is that it begs the question. It is not possible to understand the history of the papacy in the Renaissance by recounting anecdotes, however entertaining, about the behavior of the popes, or recording unsystematically evidence of abuses and corruption in the church. Nor, to explain its failure to meet the religious and social crises of the day, is it sufficient to attack piecemeal specific policies of the papacy—e.g., its involvement in the politics and wars of Italy, its interest in Renaissance culture, or preoccupation with the materialistic bases of power (rents, taxes, administration, etc.). The historian, of course, must not ignore the influence of personality or problems of morality, and cannot avoid reconstructing in detail the reactions of the popes to the various challenges which confronted the church. But to determine the significance of individual behavior, or the validity of a specific policy and the priority it ought to have received, we need to view these in the context of the time. One must first take into account the papacy's own understanding of what it was about. To do this it is necessary to identify those basic assumptions and ideals which together comprised the hierarchy of values in terms of which the popes constructed their aims and objectives, formulated their policies, and weighed their commitments.

In approaching the subject from this angle it should be understood that it is not our intention to justify. The complicity of the Renaissance papacy in the breakup of the church is a matter of record which no amount of explaining can eradicate. Our problem then is to understand the basis for the course of action, or inaction, as the case may be, which the popes followed. For this purpose it is not enough to evaluate their record with an alien set of standards—whether that of their humanist critics, or of Luther, or of the modern historian. To make sense out of the responses of the popes to the problems of the Renaissance one must also see things from the papal point of view.

The confusion caused by approaching the subject from the wrong direction is readily apparent in the case of Pius II. He is the best known and most popular of the Renaissance popes. He is also the most controversial. Pius was at one with the other popes of the Renaissance in his assessment of the major needs of the church. Indeed there was a remarkable degree of continuity in policy from Martin V (1417–1431) through Leo X. Individual popes, of course, emphasized or gave higher priority to different aspects of the total program. But all were committed to certain fundamental aims: (1) reestablishing in principle and practice the supreme authority of the pope over the whole church in face of those who argued for the higher authority of a general council; (2) recovering territory in Italy which formerly comprised the papal states and which had served as a source of material support for the church as well as providing the papacy with a home free from the authority of any secular prince; (3) extirpating heresy and imposing a uniformity of belief and religious practice throughout Christendom; and (4) defending the faith against the advance of Islam by promoting the crusade to drive the Turks out of Europe.

Even before becoming pope, as humanist scholar and secretary, as councillor and diplomat in the service of church prelates and lay princes, Pius (then Aeneas Sylvius Piccolomini) had labored in behalf of the cause of Christian unity. Particularly in the employ of the Holy Roman Emperor, Frederick III, he had worked for peace among Christian rulers, obedience to Rome, and a common front against the Turks. It was to these ends that he also dedicated himself as pope. Above all Pius believed that the very existence of Christendom was threatened by the victories of the Ottomans. Only a century earlier the Turks had crossed from Asia Minor into Greece. Now they were firmly established in Europe and had made Constantinople their capital. They had absorbed most of the Balkan peninsula, the islands of the Aegean Sea, and were already attacking Hungary and raiding into Germany. Pius, together with many contemporaries, believed that unless they were stopped the Turks would conquer all Europe and stamp out the Christian religion. At the opening of his pontificate he announced his intention of doing everything in his power to bring peace among Christians and carry the war against the Turks. The crusade, then, was the overriding concern of Pius II; it is also the key to understanding his pontificate.

The efforts of Pius to promote the unity and defense of Christendom may be quickly indicated. On October 13, 1458, the pope issued a call for an European congress which was to meet in Mantua the following year and over which the pope himself presided. He seized every opportunity to discuss the problem with the members of the papal court and the representatives of the western powers. He also negotiated with eastern princes, both Christian and pagan, who sent embassies to Rome. He publicized his cause by his own letters and treatises. He dispatched legates, preachers, and sellers of indulgences throughout Europe. He sent the ambassadors of eastern potentates and also captive Turks on tours to

stimulate interest in the West. He received and employed in similar fashion Christian rulers whose lands had fallen to the Turks.
On one occasion he staged a huge public demonstration to welcome
a sacred relic, the head of the Apostle St. Andrew, brought to Rome
by an exiled ruler from Greece. Pius gave what material support
he could to the Christian powers already under attack by the
Moslems. He founded two new knightly-military orders to fight the
Turks, as well as aiding the ancient crusading order, the Knights
of St. John, to defend its headquarters on the island of Rhodes.
Pius also placed some hope in an alleged half-brother of the Turkish
sultan, an adventurer named Bayezid Tchelebi. By advancing the
claims of this pretender the pope hoped to embarrass the sultan,
sow dissension among the Turks, and eventually convert his
enemies to Christianity. When all these means failed, Pius II, in-
firm and aged beyond his years, decided to lead the crusade himself
and thereby shame the princes and warriors of the West into joining him. On June 18, 1464, Pius took the cross in St. Peter's and
proceeded to the Italian port of Ancona where he planned to await
the arrival of volunteers. He got no farther. On August 13, 1464,
Pope Pius II died. In his last words, spoken to Cardinal Jacopo
Ammanati, he charged his devoted friend to "keep the continuation
of our holy enterprise in the mind of the brethren, and aid it with
all your power. Woe unto you, woe unto you, if you desert God's
work."

After all his pleas, the congresses and interminable negotiations,
aid actually sent to support the war against the Turks, and the
pope's own death at Ancona, Pius' commitment to the crusade, his
motives and his integrity are yet questioned by historians. By some
he has been branded a naive visionary for prosecuting a policy
which was impractical and unrealistic in the world of Renaissance
politics. At the other extreme he has been accused of using the
crusade as a political dodge in order to gain power and wealth at
the expense of the princes and for the advancement of his own
selfish interests. And even when he was credited with harboring
good intentions he has been charged with undermining them
through a conflict of interests.

Let us examine each of these charges. With the aid of the pope's
own testimony, however, we shall go beyond mere refutation.
From his letters, speeches, and his *Commentaries* (a stream-of-
consciousness account of his thought, feelings, and actions as

pope), it is possible to discover the ideals and assumptions which fitted into his policy decisions. In reconstructing the rationale of his pontificate the *Commentaries* are especially significant. Since Pius never found time to edit the work beyond the first book, and since that assignment was taken lightly by his secretary Campano, the *Commentaries* have come down to us pretty much in the form of a hurriedly written first draft revealing much more than Pius realized or ever intended.

From our point of view and with the advantage of hindsight it may appear that Pius was a visionary not only in respect to the crusade, but that all the objectives of the papal program were unrealistic. It should not be surprising to find that Pius would not agree with us. To him the objectives of the Renaissance papacy— Christian concord and unity, uniformity of belief, obedience to the Vicar of Christ, and victory over the infidel—were *real* in that they were in accordance with God's intentions as revealed to the church. And because they were conceived to be the will of God Pius believed that they would be realized, though only through strenuous efforts. Thus at the highest level, he viewed it as the responsibility of the papacy to look after the defense of the whole of Christendom. And he regarded it as the duty of all Christian princes to join in that effort. We can add that although they frequently acted otherwise, in theory at least most rulers agreed with him. At any rate Pius had no doubt about his authority to recall the princes to their duty. "What authority is higher, what dignity more sublime, what power more exalted than that of Christ's Vicar?" he wrote of his office.

While working toward these ultimate goals, Pius was compelled to set intermediate objectives. In this he was, in our terminology, *realistic*. Believing that the West was faced with imminent peril, he was ready to accept whatever help he could get in order to take immediate action. His pragmatic disposition is clearly expressed in an address to the ambassadors of the duke of Burgundy who, appearing before him at the Congress of Mantua, argued for elaborate but time-consuming preparations before marching against the Turks. Pius acknowledged the desirability of solving all problems at home and facing the Turks with a common front; but he concluded that

all this would take time; ambassadors would have to be sent and the contestants would have to be sounded, persuaded, and skillfully handled; for how could the enmities of years be dispelled in a few days? Meantime

the Hungarians, who were now nearly exhausted by war, would perish.
The Turks were already threatening them and in the coming summer they
would without doubt attack with all their might. If Hungary surrendered
to the Turks, the door was wide open into Germany and Italy and their
strength was almost doubled. There could be no doubt that if the Hungarians were deserted by the other Christians, they would be wiped out
or would ally themselves with the enemy. Either event would be fatal. . . .
(*Commentaries*, III, 214.)

Although he entertained hopes beyond the immediate defense
of Hungary, Pius was *realist* enough to admit that "we must do
what we can, not what we wish." In his own account of the negotiations at Mantua he stated concisely the guiding principles of his
policy decisions. In plain language he declared that "the greater
evil is always the one to be faced first." At Mantua he called first
for quick, decisive action to save Hungary. While the grand crusade
to expel the Turks remained his ultimate objective, he acknowledged: "Empires are won by perseverance, courage, and wisdom;
by idleness, cowardice, and ignorance they are lost." (*Commentaries*, III, 213, 223, 255.)

No doubt the realistic approach of Pius, exemplified in such
epigrams, has lent weight to the contrary charge that the pope was
a political opportunist who used the crusade to advance his power
in the West. In emphasizing expedience and decisiveness as essential to success in political undertakings and in stating his case
in maxims of a general nature Pius bears a striking resemblance to
Machiavelli. When he writes: "No steel is so good as a sword for
digging out gold"; or "He is a fool who thinks people can be persuaded to noble deeds unless it is to their material advantage";
and "It is arms that make the king or captive"; or again "In matters
carried on from a distance there is abundant opportunity for de-
ception and truth can seldom be discovered," we seem to have
entered the thought world of the famous Florentine. (*Commentaries*, III, 271; V, 374; XII, 776, 801.)

Probably no western ruler had a wider view of the contemporary
political scene than did Pius II. While still a secretary and diplomat
he had traveled extensively in Europe; he knew many of the
princes personally, and he had been directly involved in negotiations concerning the major issues of his time. Moreover, the humanist scholar had supported experience with research and study,
a habit he continued throughout his reign as pope. Possessing an

insatiable curiosity, astute powers of observation, and an uncanny memory he was uniquely qualified to exploit the intelligence which flowed into Rome from every quarter. Pius correctly predicted that the subjugation of the Balkan kingdom of Bosnia by the Turks would increase the vulnerability of Hungary and expose the Dalmatians, Croatians, Istrians, and Italians to Ottoman raiders. He foresaw that the conquest of Hungary would open the door to Vienna. He recognized that the Venetian fleet held the key to the sea passage west and that Italy was safe from attack by sea unless, as happened in 1480, Venice were found negligent.

Together with the knowledge of the international situation, the pope had a firm grasp of political realities in the West. While he continually reminded the princes of their duty as Christians he never failed to appeal to them on the basis of their individual temporal interests. He did not deceive himself about the behavior of sovereign powers. In a conference with a Florentine ambassador, in which the latter had protested that it would be better to let the Venetians face the Turks alone and thus free Italy from two threats, Pius acknowledged the aggressive character of the Venetians. "We admit," he declared, "that the Venetians, as is the way of men, covet more than they have; that they aim at the dominion of Italy and all but dare to aspire to the mastery of the world. But if the Florentines should become the equals of the Venetians in power, they would also have an equal ambition for empire. It is a common fault that no one is satisfied with his lot. No state's lands are broad enough." In the same discussion he observed: "The princes of this world and governors of cities care not by whatsoever means they protect their power so long as they protect it, and therefore they often violate the law of nations and act contrary to honorable practice." (*Commentaries,* XII, 814.)

But while he recognized such practices he most certainly did not countenance them. Pius II was no advocate of a secular doctrine of power politics. In the same dialogue with the Florentine ambassador, Pius made it abundantly clear that what people allowed or men praised in the behavior of secular princes would not be acceptable in that of a priest or pope; and that while the princes' pursuit of selfish interests had become the norm in western politics, such behavior was not in conformity with Christian ideals and was unacceptable in the eyes of the church. In the last analysis the pope's concern with the affairs of state was anchored in religion. It was in the name of religion that he summoned the princes to their duty—whether to establish peace and order within Christendom, do justice within their own dominions, or defend the faith against Islam. For Pius the fundamental issue at stake in the war against the Turks was the defense of the Gospel: "No Christian who deserves the name would prefer the rule of the Turks under which the sacraments of the church must finally be doomed and the gate to the other life be closed. . . . The victory of the Turks means the overthrow of the Gospel, which we are bound to try with all our might to prevent."

In the end Pius acted on what he regarded as the highest reality, that of faith. In taking the cross and journeying to Ancona he hoped to inspire or embarrass the princes into joining him. But, as tens of thousands before him, he became a crusader because he believed God willed it. Announcing his decision to the cardinals he declared:

An unavoidable war with the Turks threatens us. Unless we take arms and go to meet the enemy we think all is over with religion. We are determined to go at once into the war against the Turks and by deed as well as words to summon Christian princes to follow us. It is not good to say "Go"; perhaps they will listen better to "Come." We will set you an example, that as we shall do you may do also. We shall imitate our Lord and Master Jesus Christ, the holy and pure Shepherd who hesitated not to lay down His life for His sheep. We too will lay down our life for our flock since in no other way can we save the Christian religion from being trampled by the forces of the Turk. We will equip a fleet as large as the resources of the Church will permit. We will embark, old as we are and racked with sickness. We will set our sails and voyage to Greece and Asia. (*Commentaries*, XII, 822.)

In view of his concern over the advance of the Ottomans, his conception of the responsibility of his office for the defense of Christendom, and the efforts he made to oppose the Turks, we can no longer take seriously the allegation that Pius's interest in the crusade was opportunistic.

In the third charge leveled at the pope he is credited with having been serious about the crusade, but is condemned for having wrecked it on the shoals of favoritism. The phrase actually used in the charge against Pius is "nationalistic patriotism." Specifically the pope is accused of having allowed his pro-Italian sentiments to influence his judgment in the matter of the disputed crown of the kingdom of Naples. Thus in favoring the Aragonese prince, Ferrante, over the French contender, René of Anjou, Pius is al-

leged to have acted out of Italian sympathies and in so doing
alienated the king of France, a potential ally in the war against
the Turks.

Without getting deeply immersed in the history and politics of
the south Italian kingdom we can show, I think, that the pope's
actions with respect to Naples were of a piece with those involving
the crusade. By this I mean that the line of policy in each case was
consistent with the overall rationale of the Renaissance papacy
and the general assumptions which Pius shared with the other
popes of the period.

To begin with, ever since the eleventh century the popes had
claimed the right to dispose of the south Italian kingdom. A king
of Naples was legitimate only when he was recognized by the
bishop of Rome. The matter at issue was clearly the maintenance
of a friendly power in the neighboring kingdom to insure the political independence of Rome. For this purpose the Anjevin dynasty
had been introduced to the peninsula by the thirteenth-century
papacy. For the same purpose they had been replaced early in the
fifteenth century with the Aragonese dynasty in the person of
Alfonso called the Magnanimous. The succession of Alfonso's heir,
Ferrante, was complicated by the fact that he was the king's illegitimate off-spring. But in recognizing Ferrante, over the pro-
tests of France and the Anjevin party, Pius was only confirming
the decision of a predecessor; and in sticking with the Aragonese
(a Spanish, not a native Italian dynasty), he was maintaining a
tradition which went back to the beginning of the century.

We can add that there is no compelling reason to believe that,
had the pope favored the Anjevins, the French king would have
joined the crusade. On the other hand the record of Franco-papal
relations—including the harassment of the church by the Anjevins,
its persecution by the French king Philip IV, its "Babylonian
Captivity" at Avignon, and its subjection to the monarchy in France
under the "Pragmatic Sanction"—were sufficient to recommend
that the independence of the papacy was best assured by alliances
with the powers of Italy.

In the eyes of the Renaissance papacy the enemies of the church
were those who would deprive it of its freedom, who would subvert
its independence by attacking its power in Italy, and who refused
to recognize in the pope the successor of St. Peter, the Vicar of
Christ, and therefore the supreme authority over the whole church.
The defense of the church, that is the papal prerogatives and their

material base in Italy, against the assaults of aggressive Christian
powers, was a task regarded by Pius as only slightly less important
than that of defending the faith from the advancing forces of Islam.
Although he admitted that domination of the church by a Christian
power was preferable to that of the Turks, both were to be avoided.
Hence, preoccupied with the Turkish problem as was Pius, he
jealously guarded the rights and properties of the church against
internal threats—whether from powerful opponents such as the
king of France or petty Italian adventurers as Sigismondo Mala-
testa. It was Pius II who issued the bull *Execrabilis,* described as
a major turning point in the history of church reform, which condemned and forbade for all time appeals to a council as having an
authority higher than the pope. With equal forcefulness Pius
battled those who threatened his base in Italy. Denounced in his
own time for waging war against these Christian foes, Pius responded to the effect that if the church were not free from their
clutches it would be in no position to fight the Turks or carry out
its other duties as commanded by Christ. "We fought for Christ,"
he explained, "when we defended Ferrante. We were attacking
the Turks when we battered Sigismondo's lands." (*Commentaries,*
XII, 819.)

It is not an oversight that in our treatment of Pius II there has
been no mention of the abuses and corruption in the church which
were the grist for its contemporary critics. Nor indeed is it insignif-
icant that in Pius' *Commentaries* there is little mention of such
matters. This is not to say that basic reform in the life of the church
was ignored altogether by the popes. Some very important measures were taken: the reform of some religious orders and a succession of missions by papal legates to various parts of Europe are
not to be overlooked. One should also credit the efforts of the popes
and other churchmen in the field of education. And certainly the
popes themselves would point to the extensive construction projects
and the "modernization," in the style of the Renaissance, of existing
ecclesiastical buildings as necessary to the well-being of the church.
But clearly such activities, with the exception of the last mentioned,
were given low priority on the agenda of papal concerns. As we
have seen, to the popes reform meant first and foremost the rees-
tablishment and recognition of papal authority, reclaiming their
territorial base in Italy, eliminating heresy, and fighting the infi-
dels.

BIBLIOGRAPHICAL NOTE: The standard treatment of the popes is L. Pastor, *History of the Popes*, tr. F. Antrobus; for our period see vols. I–V (London, 1891–98). An introduction to the subject may be found in *The New Cambridge Modern History, Vol. I: The Renaissance*, ed. G. R. Potter (Cambridge, 1961), in the chapter entitled "The Papacy and the Catholic Church" by R. Aubenas. Professor Aubenas also wrote with R. Ricard, *L'Église et la Renaissance, 1449–1517* (Paris, 1951). The most recent biography of Pius II in English is R. J. Mitchell, *The Laurels and the Tiara. Pope Pius II, 1458–1464* (London, 1962). For those who read Italian G. Paparelli, *Enea Silvio Piccolomini* (Bari, 1950), is recommended. There is an abridgment of *The Commentaries* in paperback: *Memoirs of a Renaissance Pope* (New York, 1962).

LUTHER AS SCHOLAR AND THINKER
Lewis W. Spitz

Emerson spoke of

scholars as "the eyes and the heart of the world." Luther was a university professor for over thirty-three years and, in addition to teaching, sent out books, as he put it, "into all the world." He was not a scholar in today's sense of the term. He was not forced to excel in a technical way for scholarship's own sake. But he was a great scholar in his mastery of the latest and best techniques, in his genuine respect for what was sound in the scholarly inheritance, in his willingness to follow through to the necessary end the trend of his thought, in his creativity and imaginative mental thrusts, and in the vigor and precision with which he expressed his ideas. He lived his whole life in a world of learned tomes as well as polemical tracts. "We continue to be disciples," he wrote in his *Commentary on Psalm 101,* "of those speechless masters which we call books."

Luther described himself to Erasmus as a *rusticus* compared with the eloquent prince of humanists. We rarely do anything out of wisdom and precaution, he once confessed, but always out of ignorance. His was not the ignorance of insufficient knowledge or perplexity as to how to act; rather it was a willingness to think and to do even without knowing the final result of thought or action, for these he left up to God. He was capable of the most sophisticated theological discourse and able to draw the finest of scholarly distinctions. Luther did not just assume a position: He took a stand. And the stands which Luther took as a scholar were equally as important, though less dramatic, as his historic stand at the Diet of Worms. His scholarly work led him to ideas which have had a tremendous impact upon modern culture.

"Learning, wisdom, and writers must rule the world," Luther observed in his *Tabletalk (Tischreden)*. "If God out of His wrath would take away from the world all the learned men, what else would the people who are left be except cattle? And law, yes, even the Word itself, are nothing without lawyers and preachers whose service God uses, as of people He cannot get along without. Where there are no people wise through the Word and laws, there bears, lions, goats and dogs possess the government of the world, and govern the household. . . ." Not only was Luther not apologetic for being an intellectual, he believed the vocation to scholarship to be a high calling, and bluntly declared that the work of the scholar was more difficult than that of a knight in armor. Some people, he reflected, believe that to be concerned merely with the word as a writer or teacher, a preacher or jurist, is a comfortable occupation compared with riding in armor and enduring heat, frost, dust, or thirst. "It is true," he wrote in his *Sermon on Keeping Children in School* in 1530, "that it would be hard for me to ride in armor. But, on the other hand, I should like to see the rider who could sit for a whole day and look in a book, even if he did not have to be concerned, write, or think. Ask a chancellor, preacher, or rhetorician what work writing and speaking is; ask a schoolteacher what labor teaching and educating youths is. The quill is light, that is true . . . but in this work the most noble parts of the human body are active and do the most work, the best member (the head), the most noble member (the tongue), and the loftiest labor (speech). In other labors it is the fist, foot, back, or some similar member which works alone, and one may at the same time sing joyously or joke freely. Three fingers do it (they say of writing), but the entire body and soul are involved in the work." (WA 30 II, 573, 574.)[1] Luther went on to relate a story about the German emperor Maximilian, who replied to critics who had complained because he used so many scribes as ambassadors, with "I can make more knights but I cannot make more doctors."

[1] Martin Luther, *Werke*. Kritische Gesammtausgabe (Weimar, 1883 ff), commonly referred to as Weimarer Ausgabe, hence the abbreviation WA; in this case Vol. 30, pt. II, pp. 573, 574.

As a student Luther advanced from the middle of the class to the highest academic preferments. When he took his A.B. degree in 1502 he was merely thirtieth in a class of fifty-two. When he took his M.A. on January 7, 1505, he was second in a class of seventeen. And when he received his doctorate in 1512, he was first as well as last in a class of one. The books which he owned reveal what an avid student he was, for he annotated and underlined shamelessly. He did this even in volumes he borrowed from the library of the Elector of Saxony. He memorized countless passages from the Scriptures, the writings of the early church fathers, called patristics, and the classics, and had sufficient confidence in his powers of recall to quote freely (though not always accurately) without checking. He was persistent in mastering a subject. At the Black Bear Inn on the way from the Wartburg Castle to Wittenberg, he showed some Swiss students his Hebrew text and commented: "I read it every day for practice."

Throughout his life Luther worked with a strong sense of purpose because he viewed his work as a divine vocation, like all other useful labor. "If God does not command you to do a work, who are you, fool, that you dare to undertake it on your own?" he asked in 1531. "A certain divine calling belongs to a good work." The calling to the doctoral and preaching offices gave him courage and comfort not only against his foes but against the enemies within, the sense of inadequacy, ennui, fatigue, and futility which regularly beset even the most dedicated scholars.

Luther, a man of many books, is not associated in the minds of men with a single work of his own the way Machiavelli's name is wedded to *The Prince,* More's to *Utopia,* Castiglione's to *The Courtier,* or Copernicus' to *On the Revolutions of the Heavenly Spheres.* His name is linked rather with a translation, his monumental work on the German Bible. It is there that his great genius for languages unfolds. In this linguistic masterpiece the scholar who knew his Latin, was a master of Greek, and very competent in Hebrew, became the creator of a new high German language for his people. In his treatise on translating, the *Sendbrief vom Dolmetschen,* 1530, he set in two statements the limits within which the translator must move:

"One must not ask the letters in the Latin language how one should speak German."

"Nevertheless, I did not on the other hand let the letters go their own free way." (WA 30 II, 637, 640.)

His creative yet faithful translation of the Scriptures was a splendid demonstration of his own principles. In the *Sendbrief* he recounted how he and his "Sanhedrin" of Hebrew scholars searched for days and weeks for exactly the right vocable:

It often happened to us that we searched and asked for a single individual word for fourteen days, three or four weeks and still at times did not find it. On Job we, that is Master Philipp [Melanchthon], Aurogallus and I, worked in such a way that sometimes we could scarcely finish three lines in four days. (WA II, 636.)

Luther combined faithfulness to the text with a desire to make the prophets and evangelists speak German. He related how he listened to the "man in the street," to women in the market and children at play to get the words of the people with just the right nuance and richness for his vernacular translation.

In addition to his feeling for language Luther possessed a mastery of the sources and a knowledge of traditional authorities that revealed not only a brilliant mind but an indefatigable scholar. Even in his reformatory tracts, such as his three great treatises of 1520, he presented an astounding array of source material. In his *Address to the Christian Nobility,* for example, he drew on the Scriptures, church history, secular and constitutional history, canon law, and the humanists, as well as on his own experience. In his controversy with Erasmus on the freedom or servitude of the will he surprisingly used more classical references than did his humanist opponent. His allusions were indirect and entered the stream of the argument naturally. His treatise was longer than that of Erasmus, be it said, but the fact remains that his classical knowledge was at any rate impressive, and it increased during his last years when under the influence of Philipp Melanchthon, a brilliant Greek scholar as well as a reformer, Luther employed his leisure to cultivate it further.

Luther's scholarly control of the sources is most evident in his work as an exegete, that is, as an expositor of the Bible. He characteristically deprecated his own powers as an exegete and stressed that if the expositor does his work properly he will not thrust himself into the picture but will let the meaning of the passage come through clearly under its own power. A typical expression in his treatment of Psalm 17, 13–14:

There is little to be gained from our translation, and even less from Jerome. . . . I must therefore at this point call upon the very worst teacher, namely myself, and I shall therefore invent a story without prejudice or indiscreetness. If anyone knows of something better, let him help me out, but if he knows of nothing better, let him judge me fairly. (Cited by E. Mülhaupt, *D. Martin Luther's Psalmen-Auslegung,* I [Göttingen, 1959], 228.)

Luther was able to handle the text creatively and with a marked independence from the authorities because he had a point of view and a principle of interpretation more clearly delineated than, and distinctly different from most of theirs.

Perhaps the most striking fact about Luther's exegesis is the vastness of the enterprise, for the largest part of his *opera* is devoted to the exposition of the Scriptures. A second surprising aspect of his work is that the bulk of his scholarly commentaries is devoted to the Old Testament rather than the New. He lectured by preference on the Old Testament and would, at a modern university, have held the chair of Old Testament studies. In contrast, Luther preached by preference on the New Testament. He habitually chose his sermon texts from the gospel or epistle lesson for the day. When he did preach on the Old Testament he drew an overwhelming number of his sermon texts from those books which he believed to offer the richest evangelical treasures, above all Genesis and the Psalms. He was less given to singling out specific Messianic or evangelical passages as points of departure than to handling the whole history of God's way with mankind, through the dialectic of command and promise, law and gospel.

Luther commented on a total of fourteen books of the Bible, if one may group as one the minor prophets, that is, the prophets whose books were smaller in bulk than those of Isaiah, Jeremiah, and Ezekiel. Of the Old Testament books he lectured on Genesis (1535–45), Deuteronomy, the Psalms (three times), Ecclesiastes, the Song of Solomon, Isaiah, and the minor prophets. Of the New Testament books he lectured on the epistles, preeminently on Romans, on Galatians (1519 and 1531), I Timothy, Titus, Philemon, I John, and Hebrews. The evangelists as conveyors of the Word, however, seemed to inspire Luther to proclaim the *Kerygma* rather than to analyze the text. To this idealistic explanation must be added the fact that external circumstances frequently dictated Luther's choice of subject for the lectures. Other professors in the theological faculty did lecture on the four gospels. Melanchthon lectured five different times on the Epistle to the Romans, a preoccupation with St. Paul that is strongly reflected in his best known theological work, the *Loci Communes*. Perhaps it was Luther's great respect for Melanchthon's mastery of Greek and his deferring to Melanchthon's theological acumen which led him to yield the key book in his own development to his young colleague.

Luther's own exegetical procedures underwent a very marked development. From his first lectures on the Psalms, the *Dictata*, through his lectures on the Epistle to the Hebrews (1517/18) he followed the time-honored method of writing short notes explaining linguistic, textual, or limited problems of interpretation in marginal or interlinear glosses, which he called *collects*. He wrote out longer, more comprehensive explanations of the text as *scholia* or corollaries. In this he was following the established medieval practice. But he gradually emancipated himself from this traditional structure and, as his confidence increased, he produced a running commentary on the texts in his later works. His growing certainty as to his understanding of the theological substance of the Pauline epistles becomes very evident by a comparison of his early and later treatment of specific texts and themes, in the Psalms or in Galatians, on which he did commentaries separated in time by more than a decade.

Luther saw that the primacy of the Scriptures as the *norma normans*, the criterion which determines right teaching, demanded the priority of Biblical studies over all other theological disciplines and over subjects such as dialectic or Aristotelian philosophy. He therefore pressed for these principles as well as for the precedence of the fathers over later authorities. He regularly contrasted (unfavorably) the subleties of the scholastic theologians with the sounder theology of the early church fathers. Early in 1517 he expressed satisfaction that "our theology and St. Augustine are making propitious progress and rule at our university thanks to God's working." On May 9, 1518, he wrote to his old professor in scholastic theology at Erfurt, Jodokus Trutfetter:

I am absolutely persuaded that it is impossible to reform the church unless from the very ground up the canons, decretals, scholastic theology, philosophy, logic, as they are now pursued, are rooted out and other subjects taught. And I go so far in this conviction that I daily ask the Lord to let things so transpire that a fully purified study of the Bible and of the holy fathers will be restored. (WA Briefwechsel, I, 170, no. 74.)

This double emphasis upon the Scriptures as norm and the fathers as early and more reliable witnesses to correct interpretation found characteristic expression in his own exegetical work. A few examples chosen from commentaries on Old and New Testament books will illustrate his use of authorities.

The true scholar does not skip. It is quite impressive to select a passage in Luther's commentaries, almost at random, and discover the care with which he has consulted the authorities and researched each word and phrase. Consider a brief passage from his second *Psalms Commentary*, 1519, relating to the meaning of that mysterious word "Selah" (Ps. 3, 2, *et passim*). Luther cites the Septuagint, the early writers Cassiodorus, Augustine, and Jerome, Aquila of Pontus (second century translator of the Old Testament into Greek), and the Renaissance humanists Lefèvre d'Étaples and Johannes Reuchlin.

In the *Commentary on the Epistle to the Hebrews*, 1517–18, then still considered to be the work of St. Paul, Luther used an equally impressive array of authorities. The church father John Chrysostom (d. 407) was especially important because of his influential homilies on Hebrews. Luther also cited Dionysius the Areopagite (fifth century), the western fathers Ambrose and Augustine, Pseudo Ambrose and the Jewish historian, Josephus. Among Renaissance humanists he used Erasmus as his prime authority on Greek. He cited Lefèvre d'Étaples' *Commentaries on St. Paul's Epistles* (1512 and 1515). Johannes Reuchlin was his authority for questions involving Hebrew philology. The late medieval theologian Jean Gerson figured prominently, and he cited as well the traditional medieval exegetical predecessors. Above all, his interpretations rested not on authorities, but upon his own linguistic and theological analysis.

Luther knew the authorities, was willing to consult and compare them, but was essentially independent of them. When he differed from them, he usually did so in a calm, academic manner, although occasionally scorn or sharp disagreement over some absurdity or distortion prompted a cutting comment. Typical of this is his response to the fathers and to Lefèvre in his corollary on Romans 5:14, "Even over them that had not sinned after the likeness of Adam's transgressions":

Blessed Augustine interprets this in the same work as follows: over them that had not yet sinned from their own will in the same way as he did. Also blessed Ambrose understands it in this way. . . .
Faber Stapulensis [Lefèvre d'Étaples], however, understands the matter differently and he reconciles the contradiction between the phrases "in

that all had sinned" and "over them that had not sinned" in a different way. But I doubt whether he does it well; indeed, I fear he does not. He says that the phrase "after the likeness" must be referred to the word "reigned", and I am willing to grant this on account of John Chrysostom, who in expounding this passage says: "How did [death] reign? After the likeness of the transgression of Adam," etc. (WA 56, 316, 317.)

Never does one find in Luther a blind or subservient compliance with authorities ancient or modern. But this independence is not marred by disrespect for them or by an unwillingness to be guided by their wisdom where their views seem to him to be exegetically sound.

The deepest theme in history, observed Goethe, has been posed by the conflict of faith and unfaith. Luther's lifework as an exegete was necessarily tied very closely to his total religious and theological method. In his exegetical analysis Luther was not interested in merely establishing critically the historical or literal meaning of the text. Rather, as a *homo religiosus,* he struggled to grasp the theological or spiritual meaning of the message. A recurring phrase is *Das ist theologische Grammatik.* In the *Commentary on Romans 8: 24-25:* "For we are saved by hope. But hope that is seen is not hope . . .," Luther observes: "Grammatically, this way of speaking may be figurative, yet, theologically understood, it expresses a most intense feeling in a most direct and telling way. For it is ever so that when the hope that rises from the longing for a beloved object is delayed, love is made all the greater." For Luther the Scriptures were inspired by the Holy Spirit in order to convey a spiritual message, therefore their basic meaning, the literal meaning, had to be spiritual-prophetic. The essential hermeneutical or interpretative principle is to properly distinguish between law and gospel, threat and promise. The touchstone of correct evangelical exegesis is whether the interpretation of a passage magnifies the promise of God and its fulfillment in Christ. The way in which Luther drove past the philological questions to get to the theological heart of the text, never wishing to confuse the scaffolding with the structure itself, is clearly illustrated in his discourse on faith in his last work, the *Commentary on Genesis:*

I shall not dispute about the Hebrew word *haschab* whether you translate it with *reputare* or *cognitare,* since both words deal with the same idea. For when the divine Majesty considers me righteous, forgiven of my sins, and set free from eternal death, by faith I thankfully lay hold of these thoughts of God concerning me. Thus I am just, not from my works, but out of faith, by means of which I apprehend God's thoughts.

For God's thought is infallible truth. So when I grasp it, not with uncertainty or doubt, but with steadfast heart, then I am justified.

Faith is a steadfast and certain thought about God or trust in Him, that He is gracious through Christ, and that for Christ's sake, He thinks about us thoughts of peace, not thoughts of affliction or wrath. (WA 42, 563, 564.)

Luther's interpretation of the Old Testament turned upon this very fulcrum of faith. Faith is essential to seeing beyond mere profane history in the Old Testament to spiritual history, the history of God's people and the plan of salvation. His interpretation of the Old Testament was not historical in the sense of a modern critical historical science, but in the sense of divine or spiritual history seen through the believing eyes of faith. Faith makes sacred history. And sacred history is as different from the profane history of the gentiles as heaven and earth, light and shadow, life and death.

He praised the Psalms as a miniature Bible, containing in the most beautiful and compact form, like a little *enchiridion* or handbook, the totality of Scriptures and a picture of the whole Christian church done in living color and form, a mirror of Christendom. There is a double sense to the Scriptures, that which is understood by one's own intellect and that to which the Holy Spirit gives understanding. For that reason it is necessary for the exegete to be a Christian, if he is to be able to perceive the spiritual meaning of the text. The *parole* of the dogmaticians on the relationship of the Old and New Testament is based upon this view of Luther: *Novum Testamentum in vetere latet, Vetus Testamentum in novere patet*—the New Testament lies concealed in the Old, the Old Testament lies revealed in the New. Christ as the Word is the key to the Scriptures. All exegetical rules are subject to one overriding hermeneutical principle, namely that the true prophetic spiritual meaning of the Scriptures can be understood only in terms of Christ. The logic of Luther's exegesis is the logic of his christology. In interpreting the Old Testament the exegete finds a christological meaning not only in the overtly Messianic prophetic passages or in those in which the hidden meaning is certified as Messianic by New Testament references, but Luther is quite convinced that the spiritual meaning of the totality of Scriptures is to be understood in relation to Christ. The Scriptures should be

expounded in such a way that man appears to be nothing and
Christ everything.

Who would understand the Scriptures must understand Christ.
Christ himself laid down the great commission to study the Old
Testament in John 5: 39: "Search the Scriptures; for in them ye
think ye have eternal life: and they are they which testify of me."
In the early patristic period St. Ignatius coined the phrase: *Ubi
Christus, ibi ecclesia catholica.* —Where Christ is, there is the universal church. This spirit pervades Luther's understanding of the
Scriptures. In the history of Christ everything is said that can be
said concerning the history of the church, of the individual, and of
the world. It can be argued that for Luther the traditional fourfold
interpretation constituted a vague anticipation of this christo-
centric hermeneutics. Thus the historical-literal sense refers to
Christ, the allegorical sense to the church, the tropological sense
to the individual, and the anagogical sense to the end of the world
and the eschaton. All wisdom and knowledge are hidden in Christ
and the exegete's task is to lay out what the Scriptures have to
tell man about Christ. The historical-literal sense is thus identified
with the spiritual or christological sense of the Scriptures. The
spiritual sense is no longer associated with the allegorical meaning
in contrast to the literal or to the historico-critical meaning.
Luther's exegesis was thus independent of the medieval tradition
and is quite at variance with contemporary critical methods of
Biblical scholarship. Given, however, his understanding of the
Word, his achievement as an exegete is a major monument to
spirited, brilliant, and industrious scholarship. His skill as well as
his integrity and conviction shine through on every page wrested
from the text written in ancient languages.

As a scholar and intellectual Luther had the highest regard for
human reason, ranking man's *ratio* as the loftiest of all created
things. Luther's position in the long and honorable tradition of
Christian rationalism has been questioned, challenged, and often
misunderstood not only by his critics and foes, but also by his
friends. Scholars such as Hartmann Grisar, S.J., or A. Lunn, author
of *The Revolt Against Reason,* or such popular and influential
writers as Will Durant, badly distort Luther's fideism into a form
of anti-rationalism, if not anti-intellectualism. Another scholar,
Hiram Hayden, in his massive volume *The Counter-Renaissance*
groups Luther with Machiavelli, Montaigne, and Agrippa of

Nettesheim as taking part in an intellectual pendular swing against the values of the Renaissance, a movement characterized by anti-rationalism, anti-natural law, anti-ordered cosmos views. But even some acknowledged Luther scholars who were sympathetic to his beliefs have done his position less than justice. Otto Ritschel spoke of his *sacrificium intellectus* in giving God all honor. Karl Heim referred to a "basic irrational intellectualism". The great Luther scholar Karl Holl assumed that whenever Luther spoke of reason he meant simply "Christian reason" and had no operative concept of natural reason. Luther is often described as having a concept of instrumental reason, which serves as an agent in determining the meaning of the message to be accepted, but not of magisterial reason, which is the judge and arbiter of what is to be accepted. This analysis simplifies Luther's position far too much.

Faith for Luther is not credulity, an epistemological short circuit of rationalism, but *fiducia,* a loving trust in God the creator and redeemer of rational man. Like the medieval theologians, St. Bernard, Thomas Aquinas, and other stalwarts in the tradition of Christian rationalism, Luther drew a horizontal line which distinguished the areas in which reason and faith are operative, and he drew it between the realms of nature and of grace. In the realm of nature, in worldly matters and in the area of human culture natural reason reigns supreme. Luther as an Augustinian knew and approved of St. Augustine's high regard for reason, arguing for its lofty position on the grounds that in judging all things reason demonstrates its superiority to them. Perhaps the most succinct statement of Luther's position on the high place of reason in the total scheme of things is expressed in the theses which he prepared for the *Disputation Concerning Man* (1536):

1. Philosophy or human wisdom defines man as an animal having reason, sensation, and body.
2. It is not necessary at this time to debate whether man is properly or improperly called an animal.
3. But this must be known, that this definition describes man only as a mortal and in relation to this life.
4. And it is certainly true that reason is the most important and the highest in rank among all things and, in comparison with other things of this life, the best and something divine.
5. It is the inventor and mentor of all the arts, medicines, laws, and of whatever wisdom, power, virtue, and glory men possess in this life.

6. By virtue of this fact it ought to be named the essential difference by which man is distinguished from the animals and other things.

7. Holy Scripture also makes it lord over the earth, birds, fish, and cattle, saying, "Have dominion."

8. That is, that it is a sun and a kind of god appointed to administer these things in this life.

9. Nor did God after the fall of Adam take away this majesty of reason, but rather confirmed it.

10. In spite of the fact that it is of such majesty, it does not know itself *a priori*, but only *a posteriori*.

11. Therefore, if philosophy or reason itself is compared with theology, it will appear that we know almost nothing about man.[2]

Luther used the term reason in three different ways and much of the misunderstanding about his place in intellectual history derives from a failure to distinguish his various uses. He distinguished natural, regenerate, and arrogant reason. Natural reason is the most splendid achievement of God's creation, the crowning glory of the world of nature. Even after the fall of man it remained supreme. Regenerate reason is the reason of the man who has come to faith in God. The outlook of such a man, who sees life as an exercise of faith active in love, is qualitatively different. Regenerate reason is freed for fully creative expression by the positive outlook on life engendered in it, for faith is a *vita cordis,* the life of his heart. Finally, arrogant reason is the harlot reason of unregenerate man who refuses to accept God's revelation and His terms of salvation. It insists, on the one hand, upon offering its own righteousness for salvation or, on the other hand, asserts that since faith saves, good works are no longer necessary. Luther regularly uses the term reason as a synecdoche for the whole man in different spiritual conditions, natural man, regenerate man, reprobate man.

When Luther made his dramatic appeal at Worms to the Scriptures, clear reason, and conscience, the clear reason or *ratio evidens* to which he referred was the reason of a man informed by the Word of God. Luther answered the emperor in these words:

Since then your serene majesty and your lordships seek a simple answer, I will give it in this manner, neither horned nor toothed: Unless I am con-

[2] WA 39 I, 175–180. Cited here from *Luther's Works,* American edition, XXXIV, ed. L. Spitz (Philadelphia, 1960), 137.

vinced by the testimony of the Scriptures or by clear reason (for I do not trust either in the pope or in councils alone, since it is well known that they have often erred and contradicted themselves), I am bound by the Scriptures I have quoted and my conscience is captive to the Word of God. I cannot and I will not retract anything, since it is neither safe nor right to go against conscience.

I cannot do otherwise, here I stand, may God help me. Amen.[3]

His appeal in this case was to the reason of regenerate man. He is not asserting the right of the autonomous individual to defy the teaching of tradition or the church on the basis of natural reason, but he is affirming the duty of regenerate man, informed by the Spirit, to let himself be directed, indeed bound, by the Word. Natural reason is perfectly capable of working very effectively even on sacred texts in order to establish the literal, historico-critical, philologically sound meaning. Luther was grateful for the aid of Jewish scholars in the translation of the Hebrew text. Regenerate reason is open to the guidance of the Holy Spirit in perceiving the religious meaning of a text. The role of reason in Luther's scholarly work is of central importance. His concern for higher culture as a legitimate sphere of faith's works, and his own achievements as a scholar produced historically a powerful impact upon western culture.

BIBLIOGRAPHICAL NOTE: For Luther's early development see H. Boehmer, *Martin Luther: Road to Reformation*, tr. J. W. Doberstein and T. G. Tappert (New York, 1957); and E. G. Rupp, *Luther's Progress to the Diet of Worms* (New York, 1964). For the complete life the place to start is with R. H. Bainton, *Here I Stand: A Life of Martin Luther* (Nashville, 1950). On Luther as translator see H. Bluhm, *Martin Luther, Creative Translator* (St. Louis, 1965); and on the problem of reason: B. Lohse, *Ratio und Fides* (Göttingen, 1958), and B. Gerrish, *Grace and Reason* (Oxford, 1962).

[3] Cited by B. Lohse in *Mitteilungen der Luthergesellschaft* (1958), 124–134.

COPERNICUS AND
RENAISSANCE
ASTRONOMY
 Edward Rosen

Long after a decisive

breakthrough it is quite easy for those who come later to glance back and say: Really, when you think it over, there was nothing to it. How obvious it all was! Why should anybody consider this man significant in the evolution of human thought? On the other hand, if we wish to have a correct understanding of the crucial epoch in human progress that we call the Renaissance, and in particular of its astronomical aspect, we must not evaluate the period only from our present vantage point. Nowadays the contribution of Copernicus (1473–1543) may indeed seem puny alongside the gigantic advances that have been made since his time. But to attain a balanced appraisal, we should also weigh his work against the ideas of his predecessors.

For this purpose it is unnecessary to recount in full detail the cosmological conceptions that prevailed until the time of Copernicus. However, to recall a few of the distinctive features of the pre-Copernican world view will enable us to see more clearly exactly what he did. First, let us ask ourselves what kind of body we live on. What is the nature of this earth of ours? Before Copernicus, it was almost universally considered *not* to be a heavenly body. The earth was placed in a category apart from the heavenly bodies. This disjunction divided the universe into two separate layers. The planets and countless stars dotted the heavenly region.

Far below it lay the subcelestial zone of the earth, on which we spend our lives, miserable or happy. This antiquated contrast between heaven and earth is still firmly embedded in the outlook of many unenlightened people, who after more than four centuries have not yet felt the full impact of Copernicus' Renaissance thinking.

This split cosmos, consisting of two disparate belts, one extending from the outermost stars all the way down to the moon, and the other sublunar, was encountered by Copernicus when he was a university student. But the more he pondered this traditional astronomy, the more profoundly convinced he became that its classification of the earth was fundamentally unsound. He realized, moreover, that many of its technical defects could be overcome by treating the earth as a heavenly body in motion rather than as a non-heavenly body at rest. This is the most drastic change introduced by Copernicus into human thinking about the physical universe in which we find ourselves. We live on a heavenly body. The upright person need not wait until he dies to go to heaven. He is born in heaven, and so is his opposite number, the downright criminal.

The far-reaching consequences of this elevation of the earth to the status of a heavenly body long dominated Copernicus' thought and conduct. He began the dedication-preface of his epoch-making treatise *On the Revolutions of the Heavenly Spheres* by stating: "I can readily imagine that as soon as some people hear that certain motions are ascribed to the terrestrial globe in this volume, they will immediately shout that I must be repudiated together with this belief." Above all else Copernicus wished to avoid any conflict with those thinkers who clung tenaciously to the old dogmas. This is the reason why he kept his *Revolutions* hidden for decades and why he refused to allow it to be printed.

It has lately become fashionable to accuse Copernicus of cowardice, politely called timidity. A leading American astronomer, who died recently, sagely observed that science in general and astronomy in particular have made enormous strides since the ecclesiastical authorities lost the power to put people to death for their opinions. After the onset of this blessed impotence it is all too easy to make an anachronistic judgment and say, as a popular writer has done: "What was there to be afraid of? Anybody could say whatever he wanted. There was no danger." Yet even in our supposedly enlightened age people in various countries are being punished in one way or another for their opinions, and in Copernicus' time the ultimate penalty could be very severe. Copernicus preferred to live a quiet life, undisturbed. Although he was driven by an inner compulsion to correct the basic errors in the scientific system that he had been taught and that was universally accepted in his day, he decided to refrain from publishing his ideas. The reaction to them, he feared, might have highly unpleasant consequences for him. Until nearly the end of his life his best friends, who certainly meant him no harm, urged him to release his manuscript for publication. They told him that he was doing his fellowmen a disservice by withholding the fruits of his labors. Deeply affected by this persistent pleading, Copernicus agreed in 1535 to disclose *part* of his work: the tables from which it was possible to predict the positions of the heavenly bodies years in advance.

One measure of the accuracy of a scientific theory is its ability to make predictions. Do we know at exactly what moment the sun will rise tomorrow? Can we say at precisely what instant the next lunar eclipse will begin, how long it will last, and what portion of the moon's surface it will darken? The science of astronomy is constantly subjected to such practical tests.

Copernicus' underlying strategy was clear. He would submit his tables to the judgment of qualified critics who, by observing the heavenly bodies and comparing their observations with the positions predicted by Copernicus, would be able to tell whether the tables were right or wrong. If the tables predicted that Mars would be at a certain position at a given moment, and in fact it turned out to be elsewhere, the most unfavorable conclusion to which any fairminded person could reasonably come would be that Copernicus was mistaken. But this would be no reason to burn the man or his book. Copernicus' plan, then, was to publish his numerical results, while keeping the theoretical foundation from public view.

But his friends were not at all satisfied with this compromise. They insisted that astronomical tables were entirely inadequate unless accompanied by their scientific explanation. Copernicus eventually relented, and his *Revolutions* was printed in its entirety in 1543.

This operation was performed under unusual circumstances. The printing shop was located in Nuremberg, a thriving commercial and industrial city hundreds of miles from Copernicus' home in Frombork, "this most remote corner" of the civilized world, as he himself called it. While the book was being printed, he fell ill. A copy of the finished work was placed in his hands as he lay dying, barely conscious. He is said to have lost his memory and vigor of mind several days before his death on May 24, 1543. In a physical sense Copernicus may have been dimly aware in his final moments that the book at which he had labored for decades—the principal production of his adult life—was at long last available to the reading public. But he probably could no longer see and therefore never realized that his treatise had been issued in a form which belied its contents.

As printed in Nuremberg, the volume began with an unsigned notice "To the Reader, concerning the Hypotheses of this Work." This anonymous notice had never been submitted to Copernicus and had never been approved by him. The propositions expounded by Copernicus throughout the *Revolutions* as physical truths were declared by this unauthorized notice to be merely useful calculating devices, whether true, probable, or false. On his deathbed Copernicus was, of course, in no condition to protest against this denigration of his doctrine. By the same token he was beyond the reach of the earthly powers who could punish him. In his case the strategy of prudence paid off. But in the subsequent generations those who were convinced that Copernicus was right and had the moral courage to say so during their lifetime ran into all kinds of difficulties. Let me cite three examples.

One of the earliest confirmed Copernicans was the brilliant German astronomer Johannes Kepler (1571–1630). Kepler left the University of Tübingen without getting his higher degree in order to accept an appointment as a high school mathematics instructor. One day, while he was explaining a certain proposition to his class, an idea occurred to him which, he excitedly felt, held the hidden secret of the structure of the cosmos. He was convinced that on that particular day by a sheer flash of insight or, as he thought of it, by divine inspiration, he was given the clue needed to penetrate to the innermost entrails of the universe. He rushed the resulting book, his *Cosmographic Mystery*, into print in 1596 with the help of his former professor, who admired him deeply and who proposed its publication under the auspices of Tübingen University.

As is customary under such circumstances, a committee of experts and specialists was designated to consider whether the university should sponsor Kepler's first treatise. This committee recommended publication, provided that the author agreed to omit the chapter in which he maintained that Copernican astronomy was not in conflict with the Bible, if the Bible were read correctly.

The faculty insisted on interpreting the Bible in their own fashion. When construed literally, rather than figuratively or imaginatively as originally intended, some expressions in the Hebrew Scriptures could be made to appear opposed to Copernicanism. By the same token, in the story about Joshua commanding the sun to stand still, the real diurnal rotation of the earth was replaced by a merely apparent motion, the daily rising and setting of the sun. This form of expression had been used in antiquity because it conformed with the thinking of ordinary people then. The Hebrew Bible was addressed to them mainly as a guide to their conduct, not as a scientific treatise embodying the results of the most recent researches.

Copernicus himself had emphasized that an ancient Christian authority, "otherwise an illustrious writer but hardly a mathematician, speaks quite childishly about the earth's shape when he mocks those who declared that the earth has the form of a globe. . . . Perhaps there will be babblers who, although completely ignorant of mathematics, nevertheless take it upon themselves to pass judgment on mathematical questions and, badly distorting some passage of Scripture to their purpose, will dare to find fault with my undertaking and censure it." The power to censure and censor was possessed by the Tübingen professors in the case of Kepler's *Cosmographic Mystery.* Since he wanted to publish his *Cosmographic Mystery,* which he felt sure contained the key to the structure of the universe, he bowed before the theological censorship, and bided his time.

Fortunately, he did not have to wait very long. In 1600 he was dismissed from his teaching post because as a loyal Lutheran he refused to become a compulsory convert to Roman Catholicism, and was named an assistant on the staff of the Imperial Mathematician of the Holy Roman Empire. Two days after the latter died, Kepler was appointed his successor. Thus, five short years after the publication of his *Cosmographic Mystery,* the obscure high school teacher had deservedly risen to the exalted position of Imperial Mathematician of the Holy Roman Empire. In that capacity he produced one of the classics of science, his *New Astronomy* (1609), in which he proved that the orbit of a planet is an ellipse with the sun at one of its foci, and that equal areas of the ellipse are swept out in equal intervals of time by the radius vector drawn from the sun to the planet. These are Kepler's first two laws of planetary motion that have ever since been accepted as basic scientific truths. Kepler's *New Astronomy* takes an honored place alongside Copernicus' *Revolutions* among those treatises in the history of science that have most radically improved our understanding of the universe.

The introduction to *New Astronomy* is superb. An eloquent and passionate writer, Kepler never surpassed the peak that he reached in this introduction. It includes a section proving that Copernicanism is compatible with the Bible; this is the chapter he'd had to delete from his *Cosmographic Mystery* at the behest of the Tübingen faculty. He added some magificant reflections on the nature of gravity which attracted a great deal of attention. Thus his proof that Copernicanism is not in conflict with the Bible when properly read, was finally printed in a highly influential book. The introduction made so deep an impression that before long it was translated into English from the Latin in which Kepler wrote it.

As the Imperial Mathematician he was beyond the reach of punitive authority, but the same was not true for two other contemporary adherents to Copernicanism. In the year 1600 Giordano Bruno was burned at the stake in Rome, and thirty-three years later in the same city Galileo Galilei was compelled to abjure Copernicanism and was sentenced to life imprisonment.

If we consider these four cases (Copernicus, the cautious canon; Kepler, the patient Imperial Mathematician; Bruno, the restless renegade monk; and Galileo, the impulsive partisan), we begin to

KEPLER'S PLANETARY LAWS OF ELLIPTICAL ORBITS AND EQUAL AREAS

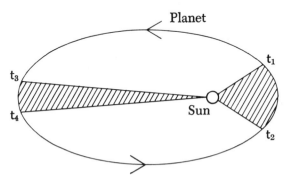

If $t_2 - t_1 = t_4 - t_3$, then the shaded areas are equal.

(This drawing deliberately exaggerates the difference between a planet's elliptical orbit and a perfect circle.)

understand the situation confronting the revolutionary intellectual
of the sixteenth and seventeenth centuries. Anybody who wished
to publish a scientific work having implications beyond the generally accepted views had to risk the possible consequences of his
thought. Incarceration, torture, and a horrible death were the
ineluctable fate of those unfortunate thinkers whose concepts
were deemed by the establishment to be dangerous. Viewed
against this background, the behavior of Copernicus is entirely
understandable.

Copernicus altered the classification of the earth, as we saw
above, so that in his system it became, and thereafter remained,
a heavenly body and one of the planets. This change in the cate-
gorization of the earth entailed an important shift in one of the
basic concepts of physics. The outstanding pre-Copernican physi-
cist was Aristotle, who had held that the earth was at rest in the
center of the universe. He also asserted that a freely falling body
headed straight for the center of the earth. If no other body ob-
structed it, it would drop right down to the earth's midpoint. All
these heavy particles pushing downward from all directions toward
the middle compressed the earth into a round ball. To the question why a freely falling body tends to move toward the center of
the earth, Aristotle's answer was that the center of the earth happened to be identical with the center of the universe. The Aristotelian earth was at the center of the Aristotelian universe, in
which earthly bodies tended toward the center of the universe.
The case of the freely falling body was so understood during the
eighteen centuries from Aristotle to Copernicus.

The latter was therefore confronted by an acute intellectual
difficulty. He had changed the status of the earth by making it a
heavenly body and a planet of the sun. He had dropped that new
solar planet into an orbit outside the orbit of Venus and inside
the orbit of Mars. But what happens now to freely falling bodies?
The center of the Copernican earth is not identical with the center
of the Copernican universe. If there is a freely falling body near
Mars, where will this Martian body fall? Will it drop toward the
center of the universe, toward the center of the earth, or toward
the center of Mars?

Copernicus' answer was that each and every one of the heavenly
bodies has its own independent and separate center of gravity.
In the Aristotelian physics the entire universe had one center of
gravity. Since Copernicus' earth was not at the center of his uni-

verse, he had to abandon the Aristotelian doctrine that the entire cosmos contained only one center of gravity. There must be multiple centers of gravity, according to Copernicus, with not only the earth but every heavenly body possessing its own. This was a long stride in the direction of the correct understanding of universal gravitation.

What Copernicus did is of course not to be equated with what was done later by the renowned Copernican Isaac Newton, who brought this development to its logical conclusion. But the history of physics, when properly written, credits Copernicus with taking a long and valuable step away from Aristotle in the direction that ultimately led to Newton's doctrine of universal gravitation.

Before turning to another aspect of Copernicus' reorientation of human thinking about our cosmos, let us note the pattern of prudence discernible in his practical as well as in his intellectual life. Having found it necessary to depart from a basic tenet of Aristotelian physics, did he, like his younger contemporary, Peter Ramus, immediately leap to the conclusion that everything Aristotle said was out of touch with reality, and therefore the whole Aristotelian system must be overturned and uprooted? Not in the least. His line of reasoning followed a more moderate course. After transforming the earth into a heavenly body and relocating it from the center of the universe to the third planetary orbit, he was constrained to reject Aristotle's unique center of gravity and assert the existence of multiple gravitational centers. But, adhering to Aristotle's distinction between two kinds of motion, natural and imposed, Copernicus classified the motion of the earth in his own universe as natural. Thus he could fit the moving earth into Aristotle's theory of motion. On the other hand, the ancient Greek philosopher's theory of gravity could not be accommodated to a moving earth without being altered beyond recognition. As a prudent reformer in the area of scientific thought, Copernicus refrained from drawing any wild inferences and propounding any unjustified generalizations. He confined his alterations of the traditional cosmology to those aspects which he clearly realized must change.

A fundamental feature of the pre-Copernican cosmology was its confident assertion that the universe was finite. The dimensions of its constituent parts were deemed to be known with precision as a result of certain ingenious mathematical procedures. Its overall size, from the earth at its center to the sphere of the fixed stars at its outermost limit, was a manageable multiple of the earth's radius.

When Copernicus raised the earth to the third planetary orbit, a baffling question arose in his mind. Once a year the earth completed a grand circuit around the sun at the center of his universe. Then a terrestrial observer gazing at the stars on any clear night should see them slightly displaced when observed six months later. For at this interval of half a year the two observational stations face each other from opposite ends of a diameter drawn through the earth's orbit around the sun. The length of this diameter, which is twice the distance from the earth to the sun, is now known to be about 400 million miles (a figure considerably larger than Copernicus' estimate). Despite this vast distance separating the two observatories, the naked eye could not detect any displacement of the stars resulting from the earth's orbital revolution. Then how was Copernicus to explain the absence of annual stellar parallax, as this phenomenon is technically known?

His opponents contended that since no such parallax was observed, the earth did not revolve in a year about the sun; it was no planet; and Copernicus was all wrong. But this objection had been anticipated by Copernicus. To account for the absence of stellar parallax, he asserted that the stars were enormously remote from the earth. Although the distance from the sun to the earth was vast, it was as nothing when put beside the incomparably vaster distance from the sun (or earth) to the stars. The insignificance of the distance sun–earth on the scale of the distance sun–stars made the annual stellar parallax so minute that it could not be perceived with the naked eye of feeble human vision. The telescope was invented not long after Copernicus' death. Its steady improvement at length enabled skillful observers to detect annual parallax in the nearer stars. The orbital revolution of the earth about the sun was thus finally proved by visual means, and a key principle of the Copernican astronomy was established beyond cavil.

The enormous remoteness of the stars was likewise confirmed. But how far out into space did they extend? After Copernicus' death, Thomas Digges in England and Giordano Bruno did not hesitate to proclaim the universe to be infinite. These later Copernicans, however, went beyond their master. Unlike these daring followers, Copernicus never asserted the infinity of the universe. He contented himself with the restrained declaration that the universe is immense and *like* the infinite. He went as far as the brink, but did not step over the edge of the precipice.

In his treatment of this fundamental question Copernicus displayed his characteristically circumspect prudence. Let us recall his proposal to publish only his numerical tables, consenting to the publication of his entire work only after he had summoned an impressive defense team featuring the reigning pope, a cardinal, and a bishop. A distinguished professor at a renowned university may insist on labeling Copernicus a conservative, and the author of a best-seller may condemn him for timidity. Nevertheless they do a grave disservice to sound historical scholarship by ignoring the dangers lurking in the path of the revolutionary intellectual, and the positive contribution made by the man who awakened astronomy from its millennial slumber. For as long as the earth stood still, astronomy stood still.

BIBLIOGRAPHICAL NOTE: For further reading the following are recommended: A. Wolf, *A History of Science, Technology, and Philosophy in the Sixteenth and Seventeenth Centuries* (2nd ed., Gloucester, 1968); I. B. Cohen, *The Birth of a New Physics* (New York, 1960); A. Pannekoek, *A History of Astronomy* (London, 1961). See also Edward Rosen, ed. and tr., *Three Copernican Treatises* (2nd ed., New York, 1959); *Kepler's Somnium* (Madison, 1967); and *Kepler's Conversation with Galileo's Sidereal Messenger* (New York, 1965).

THE PAIDEIA OF A RENAISSANCE GENTLEMAN: CASTIGLIONE'S *BOOK OF THE COURTIER*

Roslyn Brogue Henning

For those who first

proclaimed it, the Renaissance was a rebirth of civilization, a revival of classical learning. But since this revival took place in a Christian age, it could not lead to a simple resumption of Greek or Roman thought. Homer stated the classical idea of a gentleman: ". . . Always to be the best and surpass the others." (*Iliad* XI, 783–4.) Greek public performances were always competitive whether they were displays of strength and skill or presentations of lyre-playing or drama. Life was a contest, and to excel meant to vanquish one's rivals. But for the Christian, the ultimate and only important excellence was attainable by all, with God's help.

Both Greeks and Christians aimed at perfection of the individual. But to the Greeks, the full realization of human potential was achieved only by gifted and persevering individuals. They called it *arete*. (The Romans translated this notion of outstanding perfection by two words, *virtus* and *excellentia*, distinguishing perfection in itself from comparative degree of perfection.) Christians, however, believed that perfection had become an intrinsic part of man's nature through the very act of God's creation. And though lost through the disobedience of Adam, it was restored to man by the intercession of Christ.

Medieval Christianity emphasized man's dependence on God's judgment and mercy so much that the search for spiritual perfection seemed to require contempt for attainments of this world. Renaissance thought did not deny man's dependence on God, but it emphasized the essential goodness of God's whole creation and the excellences attainable through man's human nature. The Renaissance chose to be eclectic. The expanding horizons of life led to a fresh recognition of the goodness of God's world itself, and from that to a willingness to rediscover and appropriate all that was good in pagan thought. At the same time a new enthusiasm for classical learning led to a greater appreciation of worldly wisdom and accomplishments. Whatever did not directly contradict revealed truth could be added to Christian knowledge and experience. Thus, for example, the Renaissance combined the Greek regard for pleasure as a good in itself with the Christian acceptance of pleasure as a gift of God.

The most comprehensive term for God's beneficence to man is "grace": Latin *gratia* or Greek *charis*. These words come from the same root, and their original meaning is the same in both languages: as a verb, "to rejoice," "be delighted"; as an adjective, "pleasing," "acceptable," "beloved." As a noun, "grace" can express either the active feeling of one person towards another: favor, good will, esteem, love; or the corresponding passive feeling: pleasure or gratitude. Or it can mean "that which is pleasing, or estimable," to give or receive; finally it can simply mean a gift. God does what he pleases. It pleased him to create the universe and make man in his own image. All nature, including human nature, is his gift. The varied talents of individual men are his gifts. All of God's gifts are acts of divine grace, in every sense of the word. God's favor, God's pleasure, and God's forgiveness are one and the same grace of God.

No systematic and explicit theory of divine grace is presented in the Old Testament or in the Gospels. The words *gratia* and *charis* are used in the Bible in the full range of meanings also found in secular literature. And as in secular literature, given instances can be ambiguous or combine overlapping senses. St. Paul was the first to distinguish the philosophical implications of grace, and he did so in Hellenistic terms, chiefly in his letters to communities of Greek Christians. By the time of St. Thomas Aquinas in the High Middle Ages, an elaborate and comprehensive doctrine of divine grace had been defined, based on studious comparison of scriptural texts and previous interpretations by authoritative teachers of the church. In the hands of the theologians, of course, the terms lost their original secular meanings and became part of the specialized language of theology.

But with the rediscovery of classical learning, the concept of grace could no longer be limited to theology. Renaissance scholars found *charis* used by Homer, Pindar, Euripides, and Thucydides, and *gratia* used by Plautus, Livy, Caesar, Cicero, Catullus, and Ovid. Alongside the medieval analysis of divine grace, the Renaissance constructed a similarly explicit theory of secular grace. The latter became a key criterion in Renaissance aesthetics. In painting, sculpture, literary style, and the dance its application is obvious, but it was just as significant in horsemanship, fencing, games, conversation, and general demeanor. "Grace" was the perfection, the excellence, to which the individual aspired in all his endeavors.

Castiglione's *Book of the Courtier,* completed about 1516, belongs to the genre of "courtesy books." It is important as a reflection of the ideals and values of Italian courtly society of that era; but its influence as a manual of manners extended far beyond Italy of the sixteenth century. Castiglione introduces his book simply by describing its origin, its intention, and its justification. He says that he writes from actual experience:

And as the savor of Duke Guido's virtues was fresh in my mind, and the delight that in those years I had felt in the loving company of such excellent persons as then frequented the court of Urbino, I was moved by the memory thereof to write these books of the Courtier. (*Courtier,* p. 1.)

From his recollections Castiglione proposed to construct a model for gentle society, and he defends his intention by appealing to classical authorities. Anticipating those who might criticize his work he writes:

. . . I am content to have erred with Plato, Xenephon, and Marcus Tullius [Cicero], and just as, according to these authors, there is the Idea of the perfect Republic, the perfect King, and the perfect Orator, so likewise there is that of the perfect Courtier. (*Courtier,* pp. 6, 7.)

Finally Castiglione commends his book to the general public, trusting that pleasure will be the natural response of ordinary men to what is good:

. . . More often than not the many, even without perfect knowledge, know by natural instinct the certain savor of good and bad, and without being able to give any reason for it, enjoy and love one thing and reject and detest another. Hence, if my book pleases in a general way, I shall take it to be good, and I shall think that it is to survive. (*Courtier,* p. 7.)

The Book of the Courtier is an inquiry into the process of attaining true excellence in human society. Pleasure is seen as a guiding principle; grace is viewed as the beginning, the means and the end of the progress toward Christian excellence; love and joy are seen as its fruition.

The structure and style of Castiglione's discourse are modeled

on those of the dialogues of Plato. Like the *Symposium, The Book
of the Courtier* consists of a series of speeches at a gathering of
friends, on topics proposed for their mutual entertainment and
edification. But the *Symposium* is a gathering of men only, for one
night's entertainment; whereas the speeches in the four books of
The Courtier are proposed and heard by a company of men and
women together, over four successive nights. In *The Courtier* each
speaker addresses the company in turn, adding to what has been
said previously, and progressing dialectically from the levels of
appearance and opinion to ultimate reality. The dialectic begins
with unexamined concepts, taking the terms as they seem to be
commonly accepted. It proceeds by distinguishing the more inclu-
sive meanings from the more specific ones, the primary meanings
from the derived ones, and attempts to order different levels of
language to different levels of reality.

Like the books of *The Republic,* the four books of *The Courtier*
treat different topics, each being an account of the speeches and
arguments that take place on a single evening, each taking up
where the previous book leaves off. In the first book, the setting
for the gathering is given in the introduction; then the good life
in this world is defined and is characterized as a condition of complete secular grace. The second book begins with a consideration
of the universal tendency to glorify the past, and attributes it to
old men who praise bygone times because they naturally take less
pleasure in the present than in the time of their youth and vigor.
In the third book Castiglione correctly predicts that posterity will
admire his own century just as men of his own age admire the
ancients. The fourth book is prefaced by an essay on fortune and
virtue, in which he acknowledges God's grace in bestowing true
excellences upon men.

Castiglione's portraits of the actual historical persons who are
his characters accord well with what is otherwise known of them.
He presents the example of a happy society, emphasizing the personal excellence of an ideally complete Christian gentleman and an
ideally complete Christian lady. He takes his example from the
court of Urbino at which he had served for twelve years. The city
of Urbino was blessed with fertile countryside, wholesome air,
and above all, with excellent rulers. Castiglione says that there
are many witnesses who can testify to the prudence, humanity,
justice, generosity, undaunted spirit, and military prowess of
Duke Federico[1] who, among his other laudable deeds, built a

[1] Federico da Montefeltro (1422–82), made duke of Urbino in 1444. See *Courtier,*
p. 381.

palace and furnished it not only with silver vases and hangings of richest silk, but with ancient statues, paintings, musical instruments, and books. It was built upon the rocks, like the house in the parable (Luke, 6:48), and it provided for joys of the senses, of imagination, and of intellect. The house is thus a metaphor of the good life.

Within this house, Duchess Elisabetta Gonzaga[2] and her friend Signora Emilia Pia[3] presided over all social activities. While they are introduced as historical persons, in the *Courtier* Castiglione also has them personify the main ideas of the book. Like Rachel and Leah of the Old Testament, or Mary and Martha of the Gospels, they represent the traditional types of the contemplative and the active life. The duchess embodies and exemplifies wit, judgment, and reason. As persons the two ladies guide the course of the entertainment; as ideas they control the dialectic itself.

The dramatic action of the dialogue begins when the gentlemen, as was their custom, join the duchess and her friend following dinner. The ladies ask the gentlemen to propose a game for the evening. After several proposals, they choose to have one of their number set the conditions and qualities of a perfect courtier. They ask Count Ludovico da Canossa[4] to speak first, and the discourse of the first night sets forth what is given and what can be attained, that is, nature and art. As yet, appearance and reality are not distinguished.

The ideal courtier, says the count, should be of noble birth, because noble ancestors are likely to produce noble descendants, just as do horses or fruit trees. Another member of the company, Gasparo Pallavicino,[5] points out, to the contrary, that nature does not necessarily observe the social distinctions of nobility; the greatest gifts of nature are often bestowed on persons of humble origin. Nature is, in fact, what is given. Some men are born with every good quality of mind and body; others are so inept and uncouth that we think nature brought them into the world out of spite. The latter yield little fruit even with constant diligence and care; the former, with minimal labor, attain excellence. However, there is a

---

[2] Elisabetta Gonzaga (1471–1526), daughter of the Marquess Federico Gonzaga of Mantua, who married the second duke of Urbino, Guidobaldo da Montefeltro. See *Courtier*, p. 378.

[3] Emilia Pia (d. 1528), daughter of Marco Pio, lord of Carpi, and companion of the Duchess Elisabetta. See *Courtier*, p. 383.

[4] Ludovico da Canossa (1476–1532), close friend and relative of Castiglione, who resided at the court of Urbino, was successively bishop of Tricarico, Bayeux; served as ambassador of Pope Leo X to England and France, and as emissary of King Francis I of France to Venice. See *Courtier*, p. 372.

[5] Gasparo Pallavicino (1486–1511), descendant of the Marquesses of Cortemaggiore, close friend of Castiglione. See *Courtier*, p. 382.

mean between such supreme grace and such ineptitude, and those who are not so perfectly endowed by nature can correct and polish what nature has given.

The count insists that noble birth is an advantage because it creates a favorable first impression, and concludes that the courtier should be endowed by nature not only with talent and with beauty of countenance and person, but with that certain grace which shall make him at first sight pleasing and lovable to all who see him, giving the promise outwardly that such a one is worthy of the company and the favor of every great lord.

The count then sets forth his curriculum, beginning with the primary disciplines which Plato took from traditional Greek education, and which united training of the body and mind with inculcation of moral values: gymnastics and military training, and music, which included not only music in the present-day sense of the word but also poetry. To these the count adds the Christian virtues of service and humility. Since the primary service of a courtier to his lord is the profession of arms, he should be practiced in the use of weapons, courageous and prudent. He should also engage in athletic sports and exercises. He should put every effort into outstripping all others in the exercises befitting a gentleman, so that he may always be recognized as better than the rest. But above all, let him temper every action with good judgment and grace if he would deserve the universal favor that is so greatly prized. In the honor and loyalty of his military prowess, he should strive from the beginning to make a good impression, but he should avoid ostentation and that impudent praise of himself by which a man always arouses hatred and disgust in all who hear him.

Then he should be more than passably learned in letters, at least in those studies we call the humanities. He should know both Latin and Greek, and be versed in the poets, orators, and historians. He should know how to speak and write well, both prose and verse, be able to read music and play various instruments, and even have a knowledge of how to draw and paint. In all these attainments he should be modest and genial, and full of grace in all that he does or says.

The speaker is interrupted by another member of the company, Cesare Gonzaga,[6] who demands an explanation of grace. He points out that by the very meaning of the word, he who has grace finds grace; that is, those naturally endowed with excellences of body and mind will be pleasing and admirable to others. But since the

[6] Cesare Gonzaga (1475–1512), of a younger branch of the Gonzaga family, a cousin and close friend of Castiglione. See *Courtier*, p. 377.

speaker has said that grace is the gift of nature and the heavens, and has also said that, if it is not perfect, it can be increased by care and industry, what art can achieve a grace not already given?

Count Ludovico replies that it must be an art which does not seem to be art. One must avoid affectation and practice in all things a certain *sprezzatura* (literally, disdain or carelessness), so as to conceal art, and make whatever is done or said appear to be without effort. Grace comes from this ease of practice, because everyone knows the difficulty of things that are rare and well done, wherefore facility in such things causes the greatest admiration. Obvious effort is the antithesis of grace. Grace, in this sense, becomes an effect produced upon others and belongs to the realm of appearances, just as does the natural superiority which is attributed to noble birth. Graceful manner and noble birth are esteemed as indications of noble nature.

But the "art which conceals art" consists of diligent observation of the good until by constant practice the right action becomes habitual. This part of the count's explanation rests upon Aristotelian doctrine which had been incorporated into scholastic teaching. Aristotle describes all the excellences, or virtues, whether moral, intellectual, or physical, as habits; and habit becomes an acquired, "second" nature. This is the aim of education. Aristotle also says that learning is difficult and painful, but to know and to function according to nature is pleasant to all men. Hence care and effort can attain the effortless and pleasing, and art can polish and correct what is given by nature. When right action is habitual, it attains the status of nature and becomes grace itself.

In the course of this first speech there are many contributions from other members of the gathering. Some lead to extensive discussion. Especially noteworthy is the discussion of style in speech and writing, in which the principle of grace is discussed in terms of beauty, dignity, copiousness, polished and harmonious order (all Ciceronian terms). Another noteworthy discussion is concerned with the moral and intellectual importance of music, painting, and sculpture. Count Ludovico concludes by saying that a knowledge of painting is the source of very great pleasure. Those who are so enraptured when they contemplate a woman's beauty and yet cannot paint would gain much greater pleasure if they could, because they would more perfectly discern the beauty that engenders so much satisfaction in their hearts.

After this catalogue of excellent qualities and what is needed to produce them, the company desired to hear how the courtier will put them into effect. The topic is continued for another evening, and a second speaker is chosen, Federico Fregoso.[7]

The second book is concerned with the actions which proceed from the excellences bestowed by nature and perfected or acquired by education. Actions are directed to ends and involve consideration of the appropriate means and relevant circumstances. It seems to him, Federico says, that the right rule of conduct consists in a certain prudence and wise choice, and in discerning what the relative gain or loss is in things if done opportunely or done out of season. Prudence selects and orders the means toward a chosen end. He defines the scope of his discourse by saying that in order to win praise deservedly, a good opinion on the part of all, and favor from the princes whom he serves, the courtier must know how to make the most of his good qualities without exciting envy thereby.

Federico takes up the subjects of the first book in similar order. It is proper for the courtier to see that he does his outstanding and daring feats of military prowess in the sight of the noblest men in the army, but if he wishes to touch on something in praise of himself, he will do it with dissimulation, as if by chance and in passing. As to athletic sports, the courtier should not wrestle, run or jump with peasants; if he does, he should do it only out of courtesy, not as though competing with them. And he should not enter in such games unless he is sure of winning, because it is too unseemly and undignified to see a gentleman defeated by a peasant, and yet the advantage of winning is very slight. The courtier should engage in other games and diversions, such as tennis, dancing, and music, as in something that is not his profession, letting it appear that he does not devote much time or effort to them, even though he may do them very well.

The courtier should never be at a loss for things to say that are good and well-suited to those with whom he is speaking, and he should know how to sweeten and refresh the minds of his hearers, so that without ever producing tedium, he may continually give pleasure. The courtier must perceive the differences between one man and another, and change his style accordingly. In conversation with his prince, the courtier should devote his every desire and habit and manner to pleasing his lord. He will not, however, be a flatterer; he will serve his prince by obeying and furthering the

[7] Federico Fregoso (1480–1541), nephew of Duke Guidobaldo, made archbishop of Salerno by Julius II in 1507. See *Courtier*, p. 377.

prince's wishes. He will be modest and reserved, observing always
the reverence that befits a servant in relation to his master.

The courtier should always be a little more humble than his rank
requires, not accepting too readily the favors and honors that are
offered him, but modestly refusing them while showing that he
esteems them highly. Cesare Gonzaga sums up this advice by quot-
ing Jesus' words, "When you are invited to a wedding, go, and sit
down in the lowliest place, that when he who invited you comes,
he may say: Friend, go up higher; and thus you shall have honor
in the presence of them that sit at dinner with you." (Luke 14:10)

At this point Vincenzo Calmeta[8] objects that many princes love
only those who are presumptuous in seeking favor and resort to
foul means in obtaining it. Another, Ludovico Pio,[9] asks if a gentleman is bound to obey his prince in all that he commands, even if
it is something dishonorable or disgraceful. Federico replies that
no one is bound to obey dishonorable commands. Moreover, if a
prince commands the courtier to do some deed of treachery, he is
bound not to do it, both for his own sake and in order not to minister to the shame of his lord. He should quit the service of the lord
if such service is sure to disgrace him in the eyes of all good men,
for everyone assumes that whoever serves the good is good, and
whoever serves the bad is bad. Another member of the company
asks the speaker how one can distinguish what is really good from
what appears to be good, but the speaker declines to answer, for
this is beyond the stated scope of his undertaking. (It will be found
in Book IV.)

Dress, courtesy in speech and table manners are discussed, and
this leads to a consideration of jests and witticisms, in which Federico propounds a brief theory of the comic and illustrates it by
an extensive collection of jokes, repartee, and satirical remarks.
It concludes with an admonition to show respect and reverence to
women, especially when some damage might be done their honor;
and this provokes a discussion of women's honor, in which Gasparo
Pallavicino asserts the weakness and depravity of women.

The first book ends with comment on the relation of beauty to
love. The second book ends with a debate concerning the inferi-
ority of women, traditionally known as a *querelle des femmes*.
The ladies interrupt this debate, and appoint the Magnifico

[8] Vincenzo Calmeta (or Collo) (1460–1508), poet, one-time secretary of Beatrice
d'Este. See *Courtier*, p. 372.
[9] Ludovico Pio (d. 1512), of the noble family of Carpi, distant cousin of Emilia Pia
and a brave military captain. See *Courtier*, p. 383.

Giuliano[10] to take as a topic for the third night the qualities befitting a lady, her education, and how she should put her excellences into effect.

Giuliano begins by declaring that although some qualities are
common to both the courtier and the lady, and as necessary for a
woman as for a man, there are others that befit a woman more than
a man, and others befitting a man which are totally unsuitable for
a woman. A woman should have a soft and delicate tenderness and
an air of womanly sweetness in all that she does and says. As long
as the difference is observed, much of what has been said about
the courtier applies to her as well. She may adorn herself with the
best accomplishments. Many virtues of the mind are as necessary
to a woman as to a man; she should also be of gentle birth, avoid
affectation, be naturally graceful in all her actions, know how to
gain and hold the favor of her mistress and of all others. Beauty
is more necessary to her than to the courtier, and she must be more
careful not to give occasion for evil being said of her. Like the
courtier, she should observe prudence, magnanimity, and continence. If she is married, she must have the ability to manage
her husband's property, house and children, as well as all qualities that are requisite in a good mother. A woman requires addi-
tional perfections for a life of perfect service.

The courtier has as his chief profession that of man-at-arms;
that of the lady who lives at court is to entertain graciously with
agreeable and comely conversation suited to the time and place
and to the station of the person with whom she speaks. She should
join to serene and modest manners a quick vivacity of spirit,
whereby she will show herself a stranger to all boorishness, but
with such a kind manner as to cause her to be thought no less
chaste, prudent, and gentle than she is agreeable, witty and dis-
creet. Thus she must observe a certain mean, difficult to achieve,
and as it were composed of contraries. She must have knowledge
of many things in order to entertain a person graciously, know how
to choose topics for conversation that are suited to the person with
whom she is speaking, and be careful lest she unintentionally utter
words that could offend him. She should not show ineptitude in
pretending to know what she does not know, but seek modestly

[10] Giuliano de' Medici (1479–1516), youngest son of Lorenzo de' Medici ((Il
Magnifico). During the exile of the Medici from Florence (1494–1512), Giuliano
lived much of the time at the court of Urbino. See *Courtier*, p. 380.

to do herself credit in what she does know. Thus she will be not only loved but revered by everyone.

Gasparo observes sarcastically that if the speaker allows letters, continence, and magnanimity to women, he might as well have them govern cities, make laws, and lead armies. The speaker replies that many women could indeed do so, but he was describing a court lady, not a queen. Then Gasparo insists that women are imperfect creatures, produced by defect or mistake of nature, which is the Aristotelian theory of generation. There follows a complex argument, in which Giuliano uses St. Thomas to confute Aristotle. For the Christian philosopher, all human creatures are equally perfect in original nature, since God created man, male and female, in his own likeness. Another then charges that the first woman, by her transgression, induced a man to sin against God and left to the human race a heritage of death, travail, and sorrows. The speaker has the final word, and suggests that this transgression was repaired by a woman, (Mary, mother of Jesus) who brought us so much greater gain that the very sin that was atoned by such merit is called blessed.

A discussion of chastity leads to another little treatise on love. Federico Fregoso says that the lady needs above all to have knowledge of what pertains to discourse of love, how she ought to reply to one who truly loves her when he speaks to honor her and gain her favor, or to one who puts up a false show of love. The game of love is a part of courtly entertainment, conducted for pleasure. But it also can be an exercise of cruelty by the woman and egotistic conquest by the man. Magnifico Giuliano counsels that true love is only for those for whom love can lead to marriage. It is objected that some women are married against their will, and are cruelly bound by an indissoluble chain unto death in mutual hatred and abhorrence. The speaker replies that since it is often not in our power to refuse love, she should give her lover a spiritual love only. Signora Emilia gives the rule for lovers: "He who begins to love must also begin to please his beloved and to comply entirely with her wishes, and see to it that his own desires serve her." A man agrees that his highest happiness would be "to have a single will govern both souls." The man and woman would be united in equally perfect service to each other.

The company agree to a fourth night of discourse to complete the discussion of the courtier.

The speaker of the fourth night, Ottaviano Fregoso,[11] begins by saying that the perfect courtier may indeed be excellent and worthy of praise, but not unless his activities are directed to a good end. He then declares that the aim of the perfect courtier is to win for himself the favor and mind of the prince whom he serves, so that he may be able to tell him the truth about everything he needs to know. If he sees the mind of his prince inclined to a wrong action, he may in a gentle manner avail himself of the favor acquired by his good accomplishments so as to dissuade him and bring him to the path of virtue. There follows a discussion of the perils and corruption to which rulers are exposed, and the help and advice which a true servant can give. Thus, says Ottaviano, the courtier should serve his master and lead him along the austere path of virtue by using the veil of pleasure to such an end. For there is no good more universally beneficial than a good prince, nor any evil more universally pernicious than a bad prince.

The final goal of courtiership is to serve by teaching. In all classic political and ethical doctrines, power must be joined to knowledge and wisdom: the philosopher must be king. For the Christian, God alone is King, and earthly rulers do but exercise God's power, subject to God's laws and instruction. The most honored of the saints were teachers, the Apostles, the doctors of the church, who carried on the work of Christ the teacher. At the same time all Christians are disciples in this life, who learn by love. The Renaissance appropriated from Plato the ideal of the educative force of love between all masters and disciples.

Each civilization has its *paideia*. As has been pointed out by scholars of Greek culture, *paideia* is more than a formal curriculum. It is education which is governed by the values and needs of the society; it seeks to prepare its members for the tasks and privileges peculiar to that civilization. Castiglione summed up that combination of ideals which characterize the Renaissance. He did not pretend to describe the average attainments and behavior of the Italian aristocracy, although he offered the example of noble and gracious life at the court of Urbino as evidence that these ideals were attainable aims.

---

[11] Ottaviano Fregoso (1470–1524), nephew of Duke Guidobaldo and elder brother of Federico. See *Courtier*, p. 377.

BIBLIOGRAPHICAL NOTE: The classic treatment of courtly society in Renaissance Italy is found in J. Burckhardt, *The Civilization of the Renaissance in Italy*, tr. S.G.C. Middlemore (New York, 1929), Part V. For the north in the 14th and 15th centuries see J. Huizinga, *The Waning of the Middle Ages*, tr. Hopman (London, 1927). For a more recent treatment of the reception of Renaissance values in both areas see Denys Hay, *The Italian Renaissance in Its Historical Background* (Cambridge, 1962), especially chapters VI and VII. The biography of Castiglione in English is by Julia Cartwright, *Baldassare Castiglione*, 2 vols. (London, 1908). The edition of *The Courtier* used here is the translation by Charles Singleton (New York, 1959).

MONTAIGNE ON THE
ABSURDITY AND
DIGNITY OF MAN
 Donald M. Frame

One of Montaigne's

attractions is his sense of this curious nature that we call human. It is tempting to say that this is what makes him "modern" or "eternal"; but he would smile at either term and might feel misrepresented. "I would willingly come back from the other world," he once wrote, "to give the lie to any man who portrayed me other than I was, even if it were to honor me."[1] So I shall limit myself to the safer statement that this is one reason why to many readers he seems very much alive today.

His remarks about human absurdity are perhaps more readily apparent than his strong and ever-growing sense of human dignity. I should like to discuss both aspects of his view of human nature, our absurdity and our dignity, in that order.

Let me hasten to say that I do not think his is precisely our contemporary sense of the absurd; in his view man is not the victim so much as the source, or the butt, of the absurd. However, it certainly fits the sense of "absurd" in the next-latest Webster (1936 edition), which lists as its synonyms "irrational, unreasonable,

[1] *Essays,* III: 9, 751 (Book III, ch. 9, p. 751). Source references will be given in this order, and henceforth in parentheses, in the text. The editions of reference are my translations of Montaigne: *Complete Works* or *Complete Essays* (Stanford University Press, 1957, 1958).

ludicrous, inept, incongruous"—all of them terms which Montaigne would gladly apply, indeed does apply—to man. Moreover, Montaigne himself uses the term "absurd" at least once to refer to one of our favorite follies. This is at the end of his skeptical "Apology for Raymond Sebond," where he quotes Seneca saying "O what a vile and abject thing is man, if he does not raise himself above humanity!" Then he comments: "That is a good statement and a useful desire, but equally absurd," and ends his chapter by explaining that we cannot lift ourselves by our bootstraps and that it is for our Christian faith alone, not Seneca's Stoical virtue, to aspire to such a "divine and miraculous metamorphosis." (II: 12, 457.)

The main difference between Montaigne's absurd and our own seems to be that he could take the comic view of himself and of man, where we seem to demand the tragic—and often settle for the pathetic. Ours would seem to him a rather presumptuous absurd, hence a rather absurd absurd. His is almost incredibly free from anguish (in any language: *angoisse, Angst,* or what you will); this is one of the really scandalous things about him; yet for all that it is not at all superficial; the impact of his sense of our absurdity was not comic. For many Elizabethans and Jacobeans the absurd seems to have been a source of cosmic malaise, the kind of thing Shakespeare sums up so beautifully in Hamlet's "quintessence of dust" or Lear's "poor, bare, forked animal." For Pascal it constitutes man's misery, toward which our only defensible attitude is anguish, and which (in his eyes) fully justifies his famous "wager" of faith. For many thinkers since his time faith has been a man's only answer; for others, like Sartre and Camus, it has been untenable. Nearly all, however, seem to have shared with Sartre a bleak, if not a tragic, sense of man's estate here below. Camus was one of the few I know of who still held to a stubborn sort of confidence rather analogous to that of Montaigne.

At this point, in relating Montaigne's unanguished view of our absurdity to that of Camus, I of course invite an objection: Montaigne, unlike Camus, was a Christian, a Catholic; with his faith, no wonder he could confront the absurd with some equanimity. My answer to this objection is that I see no vital relation between his faith—sincere though I am convinced it was—and many of his key convictions and attitudes, including his sense of our absurdity and his lack of distress over it.

What elements can we distinguish in Montaigne's sense of human absurdity? I would list four.

1. The precariousness of our lot; the inevitability of death.
2. Our inconsistency.
3. Our incapacity for true knowledge.
4. Our inability to achieve what we aspire to and imagine. `

Let me illustrate each of these in Montaigne's own words.

The first, the precariousness of our lot and the inevitability of death, is a favorite subject of the early essays, as we see from some of the titles: "That Our Happiness Must Not Be Judged until after Our Death" (I: 19), "Of Judging of the Death of Others" (II: 13), and especially "That to Philosophize Is to Learn to Die" (I: 20), where Montaigne talks in this vein:

> The goal of our career is death. It is the necessary object of our aim. (P. 57.) It is uncertain where death awaits us; let us await it everywhere. Premeditation of death is premeditation of freedom. . . . Since my earliest days, there is nothing with which I have occupied my mind more than with images of death. (P. 60.)

While these are not especially original insights on Montaigne's part, the fact remains that in much of his earliest thinking and writing in the *Essays* this theme is very much there.

Element number two, our inconsistency, is long a matter of concern for Montaigne. To digress for a moment on diversity in general: In one early chapter, "Of the Inequality That Is between Us" (I: 42, 189), he writes that "there is more distance from a given man to a given man than from a given man to a given animal." In the chapter that most concerns us right now, "Of the Inconsistency of Our Actions" (II: 1, 244), he writes that "there is as much difference between us and ourselves as between us and others." This chapter is full of such observations: "We are all patchwork, and so shapeless and diverse in composition that each bit, each moment, plays its own game." At times he is almost lyrical about it:

> Our ordinary practice is to follow the inclinations of our appetite, to the left, to the right, uphill and down, as the wind of circumstance carries us. We think of what we want only at the moment we want it, and we change like that animal which takes the color of the place you set it on. What we have just now planned, we presently change, and presently again we retrace our steps: nothing but oscillation and inconsistency. . . . We do not go; we are carried away, like floating objects, now gently, now violently,

according as the water is angry or calm. . . . Every day a new fancy, and our humors shift with the shifts in the weather. (P. 240.)

Note that when he says "we," he means it; his own experience is his best proof:

Not only does the wind of accident move me at will, but, besides, I am moved and disturbed as a result merely of my own unstable posture; and anyone who observes carefully can hardly find himself twice in the same state. I give my soul now one face, now another, according to which direction I turn it. If I speak of myself in different ways, that is because I look at myself in different ways. All contradictions may be found in me by some twist and in some fashion. Bashful, insolent; chaste, lascivious; talkative, taciturn; tough, delicate; clever, stupid; surly, affable; lying, truthful; learned, ignorant; liberal, miserly, and prodigal: all this I see in myself to some extent according to how I turn; and whoever studies himself really attentively finds in himself, yes, even in his judgment, this gyration and discord. I have nothing to say about myself absolutely, simply, and solidly, without confusion and without mixture, or in one word. *Distinguo* is the most universal member of my logic. (II: 1, 242.)

As element number three of our absurdity I listed our incapacity for true knowledge. Here I would point to almost the entire "Apology for Raymond Sebond" (II: 12), home of the famous *Que sçay-je?* ("What do I know?"), main expression of Montaigne's skepticism, whose two principal parts are demonstrations that man *has* no knowledge and *can have* no knowledge. To be sure, it is about man without divine grace that Montaigne undertakes to prove this; but much of his demonstration applies to all men. Considering what we have learned, and noting what he calls the "clatter of so many philosophical brains" (P. 383), he concludes that "Anyone who shrewdly gleaned an accumulation of the asininities of human wisdom would have wonders to tell." (P. 408.) (In a later chapter he remarks: "It is not our follies that make me laugh, it is our wisdoms." [III: 625.]) Considering the relativity of the best human opinion, in time and place, the inadequacy and deceptiveness of the senses, the arbitrariness of the soul, and our limitations as creatures of flux, Montaigne concludes that if by any chance we are ever right, if we are even for a moment "in the truth," we cannot possibly be sure when that moment comes. (We are somewhat like a clock that has stopped, only worse: It will be right twice a day, but you can't tell when—at least by that clock. We may not even be that.)

The fourth element in Montaigne's sense of our absurdity is the enormous discrepancy between our achievement and our imagination and aspiration. Here, to start, is just one comment out of many on our lofty notion of ourselves and our powers:

Presumption is our natural and original malady. The most vulnerable and frail of all creatures is man, and at the same time the most arrogant. He feels and sees himself lodged here, amid the mire and dung of the world, nailed and riveted to the worst, the deadest, and the most stagnant part of the universe, on the lowest story of the house and the farthest from the vault of heaven . . . ; and in his imagination he goes planting himself above the circle of the moon, and bringing the sky down beneath his feet. It is by the vanity of this same imagination that he equals himself to God, attributes to himself divine characteristics, picks himself out and separates himself from the horde of other creatures, carves out their shares to his fellows and companions the animals, and distributes among them such portions of faculties and powers as he sees fit. (II: 12, 330–31.)

Our limited power to achieve what we will or aspire to is a theme dear to Montaigne. His favorite example of the impotence of our will (I: 21, 72–73) is what he calls the "unruly liberty" of the male member, which he accuses of "obtruding so importunately when we have no use for it, and failing so importunately when we have the most use for it, and struggling for mastery so imperiously with our will. . . ." But he takes off from this to show that every part of the body is subject to similar involuntary or anti-voluntary action. "We do not command our hair to stand on end or our skin to shiver with desire or fear. . . . The tongue is paralyzed, and the voice congealed, at their own time." Worse yet, our very will is seditious: "Does it always will what we would will it to will? Doesn't it often will what we forbid it to will . . . ? Is it any more amenable than our other parts to the decisions of our reason?"

Even our power of aspiration is limited in that it cannot easily be wholehearted. Most of what generally passes for repentance, as the chapter with that title (III: 2) amply shows, is something else; much of it is mere sham. The crux of the matter is that we cannot even aspire to be very different from what we are: "It is by a similar vanity that we wish to be something other than we are. The object of such a desire does not really affect us, inasmuch as the desire contradicts and hinders itself within." (II: 3, 254.)

This fourth element, centering in presumption, is always a favorite object of Montaigne's ironic scrutiny. At times he portrays it rather straightforwardly, as in his lovely comparison (II: 12, 370) of men of learning to ears of wheat: "They rise high and lofty, heads erect and proud, as long as they are empty; but when they are full and swollen with grain in their ripeness, they begin to grow humble and lower their horns." More often he is humorous, as when his own book, that record of his thoughts, puts him in mind of a gentleman he knew "who [he says] gave knowledge of his life only by the workings of his belly; you would see on display at his home a row of chamber pots, seven or eight days' worth. That was his study, his conversation; *tout autre propos luy puoit* — all other talk stank in his nostrils." (III: 9, 721.) Sometimes he is simply comic, as in this sketch, a favorite of mine, of "a councillor of my acquaintance who, after disgorging a boatload of paragraphs with extreme effort and equal ineptitude, retired from the council chamber [of the Parlement of Bordeaux] to the urinal, where he was heard muttering very conscientiously between his teeth: *Non nobis, Domine, non nobis, sed nomini tuo da gloriam.* — 'Not unto us, O Lord, not unto us, but unto thy name give glory.'" (III: 10, 782.) We're all in that one, aren't we?

To sum up this part of the picture: Montaigne reveals man in the nakedness of his absurdity. Our lot is unenviable; death is always waiting; meanwhile we have more to fear than to hope for: as he puts it once (II: 12, 364), "Our well-being is but the privation of being ill." The contrast between our puny powers and our presumptuous notions and aspirations makes us ridiculous indeed, and makes Montaigne prefer the laughter of Democritus to the tears of Heraclitus (in the chapter named after them: I: 50, 221) because the laughter is more disdainful: "I do not think there is as much unhappiness in us as vanity, nor as much malice as stupidity. We are not so full of evil as of inanity; we are not as wretched as we are worthless." Or, to quote at length the eloquent conclusion of the chapter "Of Vanity" (III: 9, 766):

It was a paradoxical command that was given us of old by that god at Delphi: "Look into yourself, know yourself, keep to yourself; bring back your mind and your will, which are spending themselves elsewhere, into themselves; you are running out, you are scattering yourself; concentrate yourself, resist yourself; you are being betrayed, dispersed, and stolen away from yourself. Do you not see that this world keeps its sight all concentrated inward and its eyes open to contemplate itself? It is always vanity for you, within and without; but it is less vanity when it is less extensive. Except for you, O man," said that God, "each thing studies itself first, and according to its needs, has limits to its labors and desires. There is not a single thing as empty and needy as you, who embrace the universe: You are the investigator without knowledge, the magistrate without jurisdiction, and all in all, the fool of the farce."

Yet—to talk about dignity for a change—it is the same Montaigne who often makes statements such as this: "It is an absolute
perfection and virtually divine to know how to enjoy our being
rightfully." (III: 13, 857.) How can we reconcile these two attitudes, or these two poles of Montaigne's attitude?

Much of it is change: change in statement which at least partly
reflects a change in attitude. Most of his statements of man's comic
limitations belong to the early essays, those which comprise most
of Books I and II and culminate in the "Apology for Raymond
Sebond." Some of this change may be a matter of strategy: Clear
the ground by the negative criticism, then build the positive part
on firm foundations. Much of it, however, I am convinced, is a
change in attitude resulting in large part from a slow but steady
conquest of confidence in himself, in man, and in life. To point to
just a few examples: His chapter title of 1572, "That to Philosophize Is to Learn to Die," is already belied around 1578–79 by his
statement—all the more significant because made in passing—that
"it is philosophy that teaches us to live." (I: 26, 120.) Where in the
same early chapter he had spoken of death as the goal of our career,
after 1588 he contradicts this, calling death (III: 12, 805) merely
the end, not the goal, of life, and a rather unimportant part of it
at that. Against his early statement, already noted, that "our well-
being is but the privation of being ill" (II: 12, 364), we may set
his late statement about God and his gift of life to us (III: 13, 854–
55): "As for me then, I love life and cultivate it just as God has
been pleased to grant it to us. . . . We wrong the great and all-
powerful Giver by refusing his gift, nullifying it, and disfiguring
it. Himself all good, he has made all things good." The *Essays* are
full of examples of similar change in outlook.

The growing confidence that produces this change is rooted in
Montaigne's conviction that man has a right to be judged as man,
not as either an angel or a horse; that while to despise our being
may be proper for higher natures than ours, for ourselves it is a
malady. We shall return to this theme with examples a little later.
First let us see what happens to the four elements of Montaigne's
sense of the absurdity of man, as he lives with them and thinks
about them. Let me take them one by one.

The first, the precariousness of our lot and the inevitability of
death, can of course be viewed in more than one way. Ephemeral-
ity can be not only a spoiler, but equally well a condition, of human
happiness. Already in a fairly early chapter (II: 15, 463), "That

Our Desire is Increased by Difficulty," Montaigne quotes Seneca to the effect "that the enjoyment of life cannot be truly pleasant to us if we are in fear of losing it," only to point out then that the opposite may be equally true, since "we clutch and embrace this good all the more tightly and with more affection because we see that it is less secure and fear that it may be taken from us." This is one of Montaigne's happy paradoxes (we shall see another related one presently): that precariousness is a condition for much of our enjoyment. Many of our delights, if we were stuck with them forever, could be our hell—witness Dante's Paolo and Francesca, or Swift's Struldbrugs.

The second element, our inconsistency, is, as we have noted, a serious problem for Montaigne from the first: how to be somebody, something more than a meeting-place of impulses. Inconsistency is of course a part or a facet of the whole phenomenon of diversity, which long struck Montaigne as one of the main facts of experience and which is an important source of his skepticism. For if there is no unity in human nature, how can I have anything worth saying to you, or you to me? And if there is no unity in the individual, in the self from one moment to the next, how can I have anything worth saying to or about myself—or you to or about yourself? Diversity is a key theme in the *Essays* of 1580 (the first two books) and indeed almost literally their final word, when Montaigne concludes the last chapter of Book II (II: 37, 398) by saying about human opinions: "Their most universal quality is diversity and discordance." (In the final version of this chapter Montaigne deleted "and discordance" and ended the chapter and book with the word "diversity.") However, after 1580, in the second chapter of Book Three ("Of Repentance"), Montaigne clearly proclaims the unity of both the individual and the race. Here is that of the individual (P. 615): "There is no one who, if he listens to himself, does not discover in himself a pattern all his own, a ruling pattern [*une forme sienne, une forme maistresse*], which struggles against education and against the tempest of the passions that oppose it." And here he is on the unity of the race (P. 611): "I set forth a humble and inglorious life; that does not matter. You can tie up all moral philosophy with a common and private life just as well as with a life of richer stuff. Each man bears the entire form of the human condition [*Chaque homme porte la forme entière de l'humaine condition*]."

Montaigne does not lose his awareness of diversity; but he comes to see unity as well. At the beginning of his final chapter, "Of Experience" (III: 13), dealing very seriously with this problem, he remarks (P. 815) that "resemblance does not make things so much alike as difference makes them unlike." However, his conclusion on this subject a little later (P. 819) shows the balance of his final opinion. "An ingenious mixture on the part of nature. If our faces were not similar, we could not distinguish man from beast; if they were not dissimilar, we could not distinguish man from man."

In short, for all our inconstancy and inconsistency, we have a cussed, bedrock nature that we cannot completely change even if we want to; and for all our differences from one another, there is also enough resemblance to make us all representative specimens whose experience may have meaning and value for one another.

In the third element of our absurdity, our incapacity for true knowledge, there is little or no change in Montaigne's conviction, but much in what he makes of it. Even in the original version of the very chapter (II: 12) in which he exposes our incapacity at such length, there are many positive points. For one thing, the Pyrrhonistic skepticism which permeates the chapter and which many consider the center of Montaigne's thought is once discussed not as a conviction but as merely a wonderful instrument for demonstrating the folly of dogmatism. This happens (P. 430) when Montaigne tells of a cocky reformer in physical science who insisted that the ancients had their directions all mixed up; and when Montaigne pointed out that they still seem to have got where they wanted to, he answered that "at all events they miscalculated."—"I then replied to him," Montaigne goes on, "that I would rather follow facts than reason." Then he continues thus: "Now these are things that often clash. . . . And the Pyrrhonians use their arguments and their reason only to ruin the apparent facts of experience; and it is marvelous how far the suppleness of our reason has followed them in this plan of combating the evidence of the facts." In other words, Pyrrhonistic skepticism is a wonderful intellectual stunt—but perhaps only a stunt.

Another positive point that Montaigne makes in the midst of his "Apology for Raymond Sebond" is that we are not at all incapable of a sort of knowledge—imperfect, yes, but still practical—and indeed of a sort of wisdom. His main proof of our ignorance is to show that we know nothing either of God or of ourselves, and then to argue in effect: "If we do not know ourselves, what can we know?" (II: 12, 418.) By implication, knowledge of self is the knowledge most available to us, and incidentally it is the knowledge least invalidated by Montaigne's skeptical arguments. Moreover, in this same chapter, self-knowledge is shown as the key to any other knowledge, since it is the best way we have to check our faulty vision and learn, so to speak, what color glasses we are wearing. We are creatures of flux, and this fact is a reason for skepticism; but, as Descartes also saw later, to know this fact is knowledge of a sort; perhaps indeed it is even a sort of wisdom. After a long discussion of how much our notions and even our judgment vary, Montaigne writes: "At least we must become wise at our own expense." (P. 423.) If we *must* become wise, presumably we can. How? The context makes this clear: by self-study. And it is precisely from this time on (about 1577–78), and—as far as we can tell—only from this time on, that Montaigne makes self-study his main occupation and his self-portrait the subject of his book.

The final development in this domain of our inability to know is another of his happy paradoxes: that one important proof of our ignorance is also a guarantee that we can be happy. Montaigne never makes this relationship explicit; but I think it is quite clear. It is the same *arbitrariness of the soul* that guarantees both our ignorance (early) and our contentment (late). By arbitrariness of the soul I mean this: that the soul, which for Montaigne has no direct contact with externals, makes whatever it will of the reports brought to it by the senses. Whenever this is mentioned rather early, in the "Apology for Raymond Sebond," it is always a proof that our so-called knowledge is inadequate; later it is a proof that we are masters of our happiness.

Here is the first of two early passages, both taken from that chapter:

That things do not lodge in us in their own form and essence, or make their entry into us by their own power and authority, we see clearly enough. Because, if that were so, we should receive them in the same way: wine would be the same in the mouth of a sick man as in the mouth of a healthy man . . . [and Montaigne gives other examples]. Thus external objects surrender to our mercy; they dwell in us as we please. (P. 422.)

In the other early passage Montaigne describes this arbitrariness of the soul more fully (P. 354), praising it ironically as a privilege of man and then attributing it anyway to animals as well:

. . . the privilege in which our soul glories, of reducing to her condition all
that she conceives, of stripping all that comes to her of its mortal and
corporeal qualities, of constraining all the things that she considers worthy
of her acquaintance to put off and divest themselves of their corruptible
properties, and making them leave aside as base and superfluous garments
their thickness, length, depth, weight, color, odor, roughness, smoothness,
hardness, softness, and all accidents of sense, in order to accommodate
them to her immortal and spiritual condition . . . this same privilege, I say,
seems very evidently to belong to the beasts.

Now, in three additions that Montaigne made after 1588, in the
last four years of his life, note the new and positive possibilities
of this same arbitrariness:

Fortune does us neither good nor harm; she only offers us the material
and the seed of them, which our soul, more powerful than she, turns and
applies as it pleases, sole cause and mistress of its happy or unhappy condition. (I: 14, 46.)

The longer second addition, found in the same chapter, clearly
shows the connection between happiness and delusion or lack of
knowledge:

. . . the soul is the one and sovereign mistress of our condition and conduct.
The body has, except for differences of degree, only one gait and one
posture. The soul may be shaped into all varieties of forms, and molds
to itself and to its every condition the feelings of the body and all other
accidents. Therefore we must study the soul and look into it, and awaken
in it its all-powerful springs. There is no reason, prescription or might
that has power against its inclination and its choice. Out of the many
thousands of attitudes at its disposal, let us give it one conducive to our
repose and preservation, and we shall be not only sheltered from all harm,
but even gratified and flattered, if it please, by ills and pains. The soul
profits from everything without distinction. Error and dreams serve it
usefully, being suitable stuff for giving us security and contentment.
(I: 14, 39.)

The third of these additions shows most clearly and eloquently
the capacity for happiness that we owe to this arbitrary soul of ours:

Things in themselves may have their own weights and measures and
qualities; but once inside, within us, she [the soul] allots them their qualities as she sees fit. Death is frightful to Cicero, desirable to Cato, a matter
of indifference to Socrates. Health, conscience, authority, knowledge,
riches, beauty, and their opposites, all are stripped on entry and receive
from the soul new clothing, and the coloring that she chooses—brown,
green, bright, dark, bitter, sweet, deep, superficial—and which each
individual soul chooses; for they have not agreed together on their styles,
rules, and forms; each one is queen in her realm. Wherefore let us no
longer make the external qualities of things our excuse; it is up to us to

reckon them as we will. Our good and our ill depend on ourselves alone. (I: 50, 220.)

In short, out of these nettles, flux and ignorance, we may if we choose pluck these flowers, knowledge, wisdom, happiness — and these, moreover, have always been Montaigne's favorite flowers.

What happens to the fourth and last of our absurdities in Montaigne's eyes, our inability to achieve what we aspire to and imagine? Basically, not very much. Our imagination is a gullible faculty which we do well to cozen if we can, and which our mind should be able to put onto a sane track:

Now I treat my imagination as gently as I can, and would relieve it, if I could, of all trouble and conflict. We must help it and flatter it, and fool it if we can. My mind is suited to this service; it has no lack of plausible reasons for all things. If it could persuade as well as it preaches, it would help me out very happily. (III: 13, 836.)

The main thing here is Montaigne's growing insistence that we learn to accept ourselves for what we are. Proper self-acceptance, for Montaigne, is not lax; far from being an enemy to self-improvement, it is the necessary condition of it. Montaigne's main basis for this view, as we noted before, is his conviction that we can be rightly judged only in terms of what we are, in terms of our condition as humans; that self-disdain is a form of illness, not of holiness. Already in an early essay he states this once (II: 3, 254): "As for the opinion that disdains our life, it is ridiculous. For after all, life is our being. it is our all. Things that have a nobler and richer being may accuse ours; but it is against nature that we despise ourselves and care nothing about ourselves. It is a malady peculiar to man, and not seen in any other creature, to hate and disdain himself." He returns to this theme again near the end of his final essay (III: 13, 852): "The most barbarous of our maladies is to despise our being."

So much, then, for the changes in the way Montaigne looks at the many facets of human absurdity. Similar changes are found in his remarks about man in general. In the earliest essays the term "human" was seldom a form of praise; his usual stress was the familiar one, "humanistic" in one sixteenth-century sense of the term, which harped on the stupidity and universality of le vulgaire, "the vulgar" or "the common herd." Illuminating in this regard are two small alterations that Montaigne made in the same chapter ("Apology for Raymond Sebond"), in the same period (the last four years of his life), and in almost identical contexts: so that although they are some distance apart (pp. 320 and 429), it seems likely that in effect Montaigne exchanged one remark for the other. Speaking of the vulgar or the common herd, he first wrote "and practically everybody is of this sort." When much later he crossed this out entirely, he added, further on in the essay, and again when speaking of the vulgar or common herd: *et nous sommes tous du vulgaire*—"and we are all of the common herd." The difference between "practically everybody is" and "we are all" is obvious, and, I think, enormous.

Just as striking is the way in which the terms "humanity" and "human" become his highest praise. An honorable man, he says, will not lie, for he wants to be seen just as he is inside, where "either all is good, or at least all is human." (II: 17, 491.) He places Epaminondas among the most outstanding men because even in the harshest actions, such as war, he always exercised "goodness and humanity." (III: 1, 609; cf. II: 36, 573–74.) The term is praise even for a god: Vulcan's generosity to his unfaithful wife Venus is, he says, "of a humanity truly more than human." (III: 5, 658.) And the idea is central whenever Montaigne tries, as he often does in his final essay, to summarize his principal message (III: 13, 857, 852): "The most beautiful lives, to my mind, are those that conform to the common human pattern. . . . There is nothing so beautiful and legitimate as to play the man well and properly."

To sum up at last. Montaigne never jettisons his sense of human absurdity. In the triumphant conclusion of his final chapter, "Of Experience" (III: 13, 849), he still recognizes it fully:

I, who boast of embracing the pleasures of life so assiduously and so particularly, find in them, when I look at them thus minutely, virtually nothing but wind. But what of it? We are all wind. And even the wind, more wisely than we, loves to make a noise and move about, and is content with its own functions, without wishing for stability and solidity, qualities that do not belong to it.

To fail to see our absurdity is to fall into our favorite absurdity, presumption, and at the same time to fail to see more than half of our being itself (III: 5, 677–78): "Our life is part folly, part wisdom. Whoever writes about it only reverently and according to the rules leaves out more than half of it." But the cure for this does not lie in the opposite extreme of self-disdain, which normally follows when man seeks to be superhuman and fails, or insists on judging himself and his fellows by superhuman standards and thus finds mankind pathetically wanting. No, self-disdain, as we have seen, is for Montaigne no virtue but a barbarous and unnatural malady. To accept ourselves as we are, for what we are, is the beginning of wisdom and the way to true human dignity. And true human dignity, for Montaigne, can — and should — live happily with human absurdity. The following quotation, which is almost the conclusion of the *Essays,* shows just how well our dignity and our absurdity live together in Montaigne's mind (III: 13, 856–57):

They want to get out of themselves and escape from the man. That is madness: Instead of changing into angels, they change into beasts; instead of raising themselves, they lower themselves. . . .

It is an absolute perfection and virtually divine to know how to enjoy our being rightfully. We seek other conditions because we do not understand the use of our own, and go outside of ourselves because we do not know what it is like inside. Yet there is no use our mounting on stilts, for on stilts we must still walk on our own legs. And on the loftiest throne in the world *si ne sommes assis que sus nostre cul*—we are still sitting only on our own rump.

BIBLIOGRAPHICAL NOTE: For more on Montaigne the student may consult Imbrie Buffum, *Studies in the Baroque from Montaigne to Rotroy* (New Haven, 1957); Donald M. Frame, *Montaigne's Discovery of Man: The Humanization of a Humanist* (New York, 1955); Pierre Moreau, *Montaigne, l'homme et l'oeuvre* (Paris, 1939). A convenient selection of Montaigne's writings in French and English is *Essays and Selected Writings,* tr. and ed. by Donald M. Frame (New York, 1963).

Contributors

DONALD M. FRAME is professor of French at Columbia University. He edited and translated *The Complete Works of Montaigne,* and is the author of *Montaigne in France* and *Montaigne's Discovery of Man.*

FELIX GILBERT is a professor at the School of Historical Studies of the Institute of Advanced Studies at Princeton University. His writings include *Machiavelli and Guicciardini, Politics and History in Sixteenth Century Florence.*

ROSLYN BROGUE HENNING is an associate professor of music and executive director of humanistic studies at Tufts University.

RUDOLF HIRSCH is associate director of libraries and professor of history at the University of Pennsylvania. He has written among others *Printing, Selling, and Reading, 1450–1550.*

GEORGE RICHARD POTTER, a professor emeritus of medieval history at the University of Sheffield, has written on Sir Thomas More and on various Renaissance subjects. He is a contributor to *The Cambridge Medieval History* and editor of *The New Cambridge Modern History, Vol. I: The Renaissance.*

EDWARD ROSEN is a professor in the Department of History, City College of the City University of New York. His work included *Three Copernican Treatises* and *The Naming of the Telescope.*

JERROLD E. SEIGEL is professor of history at Princeton University and is the author of *Rhetoric and Philosophy in Renaissance Humanism.*

LEWIS W. SPITZ, professor of history at Stanford University, has edited a volume in the American edition of Luther's works. His writings include *Religious Renaissance of the German Humanists* and *The Reformation—Material or Spiritual.*

THE EDITOR: ROBERT SCHWOEBEL is professor of history at Temple University, and the author of *The Shadow of the Crescent: The Renaissance Image of the Turk.*